Catholic Faith Teaching Manual

Level 2 : Post Communion Level

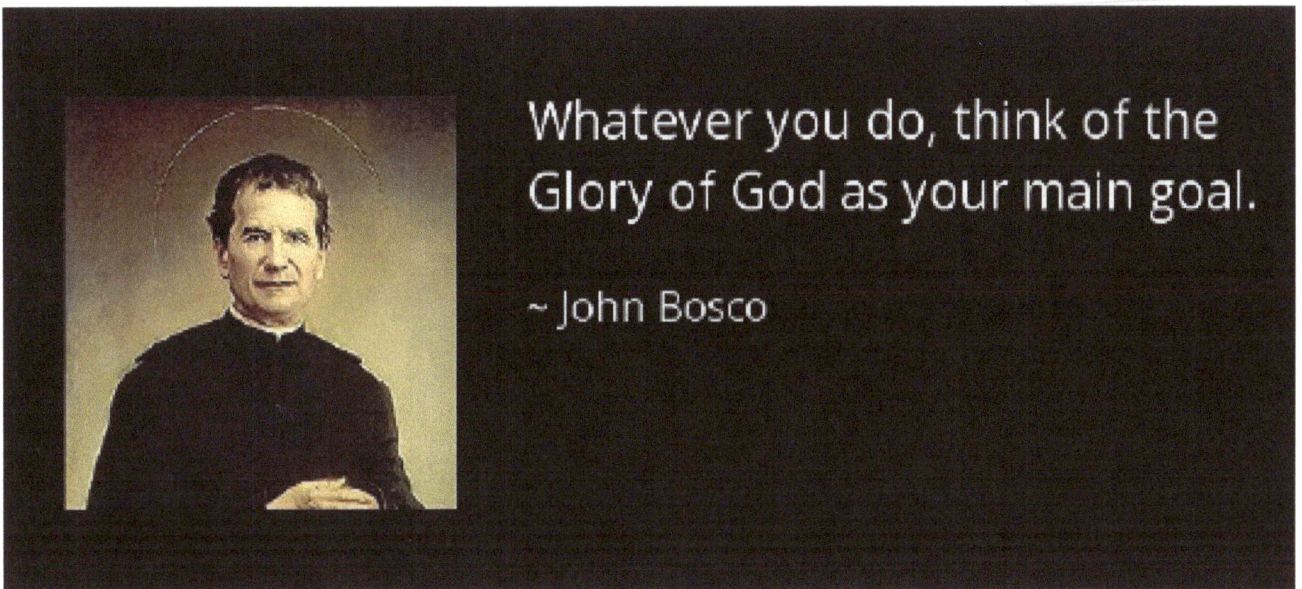

Copyright © 2020 by Father Raymond Taouk. All rights reserved.

"No part of this publication may be reproduced, distributed, or transmitted in any form or by any means, including photocopying, recording, or other electronic or mechanical methods, or by any information storage and retrieval system without the prior written permission of the publisher, except in the case of very brief quotations embodied in critical reviews and certain other noncommercial uses permitted by copyright law."

Co published with JMJ Catholic products.
www.jmjcatholicproducts.com.au
Email : jeanette@jmjcatholicproducts.com.au

ISBN: 9780645021912

TABLE OF CONTENTS

Page

Lesson 1	Catechism Questions 1, 2, 3	9
	Prayer : Grace before meals	10
	Bible	11
	Bible Story : Joseph hated by his brothers	12
	The Saints : Saint John Bosco	14
	The Rosary	16
	The history of the Rosary	17
	General : The Chasuble	18
Lesson 2	Catechism : The main purpose of mans existence (Questions 4, 5, 6, 7)	22
	Prayer : Grace after meals	24
	Bible Story : Joseph in prison	25
	The Saints : Saint Patrick	26
	The Rosary : Joyful, Sorrowful and Glorious	28
	How to say the Rosary	29
	General : The Chasuble	30
Lesson 3	Catechism : God and his perfections (Questions 8, 9, 10)	34
	Prayer : The decade Prayer	35
	Bible Story : Pharaohs Dream	36
	The Saints : Saint Christopher	38
	The Rosary : first and second Joyful mysteries	40
	General : The Biretta	41
Lesson 4	Catechism : God and His Perfections (Questions 11, 12, 13)	44
	Prayer : Act of Contrition	45
	Bible Story : The Famine	46
	The Saints : Saint John Vianney	48

		Page
Lesson 4	The Rosary : The Third Joyful Mystery	50
	General : The Communion Plate	51
Lesson 5	Catechism : The Unity and Trinity of God (Questions 14, 15, 16)	54
	Prayer : The Angelus	55
	Bible : The Story of Moses (Part 1)	56
	The Saints : Saint Bernadette	58
	The Rosary : fourth and fifth Joyful mysteries	60
	General : The Altar	61
Lesson 6	Catechism : Creation and the Angels (Questions 17, 18, 19, 20)	64
	Prayer : The Regina Coeli	65
	Bible Story : The Story of Moses (Part 2)	66
	The Saints : Saint Veronica	68
	The Rosary : first and second Sorrowful mysteries	70
	General : The Tabernacle	71
Lesson 7	Catechism : Creation and the Angels (Questions 21, 22, 23)	74
	Prayer : Apostles Creed	75
	Bible Story : The Story of Moses (Part 3)	76
	The Saints : Saint Simon of Cyrene	78
	The Rosary : third and fourth sorrowful mysteries	80
	General : Holy Water	81
Lesson 8	Catechism : The Creation and Fall of Man (Questions : 24, 25, 26, 27)	84
	Prayer : Hail Holy Queen	85
	Bible Story : The Golden Calf	86
	The Saints : Saint Thomas Aquinas	88
	The Rosary : fifth Sorrowful mystery	90

		Page
Lesson 8	General : The Seven Corporal works of Mercy	91
Lesson 9	Catechism : The Creation and the fall of man.	
	(Questions 28, 29, 30, 31)	94
	Prayer : The Pardon Prayer	95
	Bible Story : The flight into Egypt	96
	The Saints : Saint Anne	98
	The Rosary : first and second Glorious mysteries	100
	General : The Seven Corporal works of Mercy	101
Lesson 10	Catechism : Actual Sin	
	(Questions 32, 33, 34)	104
	Prayer : The Fatima Prayer to the Holy Trinity	105
	Bible Story : Jesus in the temple	106
	The Saints : Saint Dominic	108
	The Rosary : third Glorious mystery	110
	General : The Seven Corporal works of Mercy	111
Lesson 11	Catechism : Mortal Sin	
	(Questions 35, 36, 37)	114
	Prayer : Prayer to Our Guardian Angel	115
	Bible Story : The Baptism of Jesus	116
	The Saints : Saint Angela Merici	118
	The Rosary : fourth and fifth Glorious mysteries	120
	General : The Seven Corporal works of Mercy	121
Lesson 12	Catechism : Venial Sin	
	(Questions 38, 39)	124
	Prayer : The Fatima Sacrifice Prayer	125
	Bible Story : Jesus first miracle	126
	The Saints : Saint Rosa of Lima	128
	The Rosary : October the month of the Holy Rosary	130
	General : The Seven Corporal works of Mercy	131

		Page
Lesson 13	Catechism : The Incarnation	
	(Questions 40, 41, 42)	134
	Prayer : The Fatima Eucharist Prayer	135
	Bible Story : Jesus calms the storm	136
	The Saints : All Saints	138
	The Rosary : The Story of Fatima (Part 1)	140
	General : The Seven Corporal works of Mercy	141
Lesson 14	Catechism : The Incarnation	
	(Questions 43, 44, 45)	144
	Prayer : Eternal Rest	145
	Bible Story : The Loaves and the Fishes	146
	The Saints : Saint Nicholas	148
	The Rosary : The Story of Fatima (Part 2)	150
	General : The Seven Corporal works of Mercy	151
Lesson 15	Catechism Questions 1 to 7	154
	Catechism Questions 8 to 16	155
	Catechism Questions 17 to 27	156
	Catechism Questions 28 to 37	157
	Catechism Questions 38 to 45	158

Lesson 1

Level 2

Post Communion Level

Level 2 - Lesson 1

Catechism

Each Lesson we are going to study catechism questions. This is the most important part of your lesson. You must learn these questions by heart so that you will come to know a great deal about God and His wonderful creations.

1. **Who made us ?**

   God Made us

2. **Who is God ?**

   God is the supreme Being, infinitely perfect, Who made all things and keeps them in existence.

3. **Why did God make us ?**

   God made us to show us His goodness and to share with us His everlasting happiness in heaven.

We are here on this earth to know, love and serve God and to be happy with Him forever in Heaven. Nothing else matters, it does not matter if we are rich, famous, or smart.
What matters is that we love God with all our heart, with all our mind and with all our strength. Let us learn from this catechism lesson to always do everything for God.

Question 1 ❖ Who is God ?

_____

Question 2 ❖ Why did God make us ?

_____

_____

Prayer

GRACE BEFORE MEALS

**Bless us O Lord and these gifts,
of which we are about to receive,
through Christ Our Lord.
Amen**

Before breakfast, lunch and tea, we should never start our meal before asking for God's blessing upon us and the food we are about to eat.

Depending on family custom, we may say our Grace before Meals standing behind our chair or when we are seated.

We make the Sign of the Cross, say our Grace and then finish with the Sign of the Cross.

Be careful not to rush these prayers like many hungry children that often do.

Question 3 ❖ When should we say *Grace before meals*?

Question 4 ❖ Why do we say *Grace before meals*?

Level 2 - Lesson 1

Bible

Each lesson we are going to present a story from the bible. It may come from the Old Testament (before Jesus was born) or from the New Testament (after Jesus was born).

Stories from the Bible are very important for us because God Himself through the sacred authors, wrote the Bible, so everything we read in the Bible is true.

Question 5 ❖ Is the Old Testament before or after the birth of Jesus?
_____

Question 6 ❖ Is everything we read in the Bible true?
_____

Bible Story

Joseph hated by his brothers

Joseph was the son of Jacob, who was the son of Isaac, who was the son of Abraham. He had eleven brothers. Joseph was so good and so obedient that his father loved him more than any of his brothers.

To show his love, Jacob gave Joseph a coat of many colors, this made his brothers very angry. One day they committed a wicked deed and Joseph told his father about it, this made them hate him even more.

After some time, Joseph was sent by his father to the field where his brothers were feeding their sheep. When he reached them, they stripped him of his coat and threw him into a pit, they then sold him to merchants who passed by on their way to Egypt.

The brothers dipped Josephs coat in blood and sent it to their father. When the old man saw it, he said "It is my sons coat; a wild beast has eaten him" and he wept for his beloved boy. The merchants who bought Joseph took him to Egypt where he was cast into prison.

Question 7 ❖ Who was Joseph's father?

_____

Question 8 ❖ What made Joseph's brothers very angry?

_____

Question 9 ❖ Where did the merchants take Joseph?

_____

The Saints

Saint John Bosco

Saint John Bosco lived in northern Italy as a priest who loved children. He started a Religious order called the Salesians, who spent their lives helping and working with children.

St Bosco had a great devotion to Our Lady, under the title of "Mary, Help of Christians. In fact, he built a huge basilica in her honor.

He could read the souls of the boys he taught. If they committed a mortal sin, he could read it on their foreheads.

Everywhere he went, there were great miracles; people were being converted, broken bones being mended, raising people from the dead and much more.

He also had many dreams, these dreams were actually messages from God and Our Lady telling Don Bosco what to do. His first 'dream' was when he was nine years old. In this dream, Mary told him that his life was to look after boys, to make the bad boys good. He spent his whole life doing this. Among his students was Saint Dominic Savio.

Don Bosco also took care of girls, he also started up the Salesian Nuns (daughters of Mary) to look after them.

Don Bosco died on January 31st 1888, which is now his feast day. He is now in heaven praying for all children of the world.

Question 10 ❖ What Religious Order did Saint John Bosco begin?

_____

Question 11 ❖ Under what title did Saint John Bosco have a devotion to Our Lady?

_____

Question 12 ❖ When is Don Bosco's feast day?

_____

The Rosary

In Level two, we are going to study the Holy Rosary in depth.
We are going to look at its history, how to say it and why we should say it every day.
We are going to see why it pleases Our Blessed Mother so much.
By learning about the Rosary , we are learning about Mary.

Level 2 - Lesson 1

The Rosary

In this first lesson, we are going to learn about the history of the Rosary and where it came from.

Over 800 years ago, a man named Dominic was born. He was sent to become the great Saint Dominic. When Saint Dominic was a young man, there were many evil men who hated Jesus and hated truth. They were called Albigensian. They destroyed homes, they burned churches and they killed Catholics, especially priests and nuns.

St Dominic fought against the Albigenses by starting a religious order called the 'Order of Preachers'; they are usually referred to as Dominicans.

To help Saint Dominic, Our Blessed Mother appeared to him and gave him a most powerful weapon, a spiritual weapon, the Holy Rosary. Our Lady taught him to pray the Rosary and now because of Saint Dominic, the Catholic world now prays the Rosary of Our Lady.

There have been so many miracles through the Rosary over the years, which we will learn in later lessons.

Question 13

To whom did Our Lady give the Rosary?

Question 14

What type of weapon is the Rosary?

General

The Chasuble

The Chasuble is the outer vestment we see priests wear during Mass. Chasuble comes from the Latin word *casula* which means a *little house*.

There are two types of chasuble. The illustration on the next page is of a Gothic chasuble which is long and flowing.

The other type of chasuble is called a Roman Chasuble. This type of Chasuble is smaller and gives more freedom to the arms.

Depending on the feast, the priest wears different color chasubles. The colors he uses are as follows :

- White → Worn on the feasts of Our Lord and Our Lady, confessors and Popes.
- Red → Worn for the Holy Ghost and for martyrs.
- Violet (purple) → Worn during Lent and Advent
- Green → Worn on Sundays after Pentecost
- Black → Worn on Good Friday and masses for the dead.
- Rose (pink) → Worn on the 4th Sunday in Lent and 3rd Sunday in Advent
- Gold → Used on great feasts in the place of white and red.

Question 15 ❖ How many different color vestments can be worn?

_____

Question 16 ❖ What are the 2 types of Chasuble?

_____

Lesson 2

Level 2

Post Communion Level

Catechism

The Main Purpose of Mans Existence

4. **What must we do to gain happiness in heaven ?**

   To gain the happiness of heaven we must know, love and serve God in this world.

5. **From whom do we learn to know, love and serve God ?**

   We learn to know, love and serve God from Jesus Christ, the Son of God, who teaches us through the Catholic Church.

6. **Where do we find the chief truths taught by Jesus Christ through the Catholic Church ?**

   We find the chief truths taught by Jesus Christ through the Catholic Church in the Apostles Creed.

7. **Say the Apostles Creed.**

   I believe in God the Father Almighty,
   Creator of Heaven and Earth
   And in Jesus Christ,
   His only Son, Our Lord,
   Who was conceived by the Holy Spirit,
   born of the Virgin Mary
   suffered under Pontius Pilate,
   was crucified, died and buried.
   He descended into hell;
   the third day He arose from the dead,
   He ascended into heaven
   and sits at the right hand of God, the Father Almighty,
   from there he will come to judge the living and the dead.
   I believe in the Holy Spirit, the Holy Catholic Church,
   the communion of saints,
   the forgiveness of sins,
   the resurrection of the body
   and life everlasting.
   Amen

The Catechism questions this lesson teach us what we must do to be with God forever in heaven. They teach us that all truth comes from God and that we learn this through His Church. Our Catechism questions are the most important part of the religion course. When we learn the questions, we must do three things :

Firstly, we must learn them by heart. This is very important, for if we learn them well now, we will remember them for the remainder of our lives.

Secondly, we must, with the help of our parents and teachers, understand what the questions and answers mean. If we do not understand them, we must ask what they mean.

Thirdly, we must live what we learn. That means we must not only know the right answers, but we must put them into practice every day in the way we think and act.

Question 1 ❖ What must we do to gain the happiness of heaven?

_____

Question 2 ❖ From whom do we learn to know, love and serve God?

_____

Question 3 ❖ Why did God make us ?

_____

_____

Prayer

GRACE AFTER MEALS

**We give thanks, O Almighty God,
for all your benefits, who lives and reigns,
world without end.
Amen**

ETERNAL REST PRAYER

**May the souls of the faithful departed,
through the mercy of God, rest in peace.
Amen.**

Just as we say Grace before meals each time we sit down to eat our breakfast, lunch and dinner, at the end of each of these meals we should say our "Grace after meals' or "Thanksgiving prayer" as it is sometimes called. Many families forget to thank God at the end of their meal, it is important to always think of Him and thank Him. It is our way of serving Him and showing that we love Him.
After we say our "Grace after meals" prayer we then say the "Eternal Rest Prayer". We start by making the Sign of the Cross, then we say the prayer and while saying :
"May the souls of the faithful departed, through the mercy of God, rest in peace, Amen" we reverently make the Sign of the Cross.

Question 4 ❖ When should we say *Grace before meals*?

_____

Question 5 ❖ What do we do when we say, May the souls of the faithful departed, through the mercy of God, rest in peace. Amen ?

_____

Level 2 - Lesson 2

Bible Story

Joseph In Prison

Even in prison, God was with Joseph, and helped him to find favor with the prison guard, who placed Joseph in charge of all the other captives. Then it came to pass, that the chief butler and the chief baker of the Pharaoh were cast into prison.

One morning, Joseph saw that these two men were sad. He asked them, "Why are you so sad?" They answered, "We have dreamed a dream last night, and we have nobody to explain it to us,"

Joseph said to them, "Does not the interpretation come from God? Tell me what you have dreamed."

The chief butler first told his dream. Joseph answered, "After three days Pharaoh will restore you to your former place. Joseph then asked him "remember me and ask the Pharaoh to take me out of this prison, for I am innocent."

Then the chief baker told Joseph about his dream in which Joseph answered, "After three days Pharaoh will cut your head off and hang it on a cross.

The third day came. It was the birthday of Pharaoh. The Pharaoh remembered the chief butler and the chief baker. The butler was allowed to return to work in the palace, but the baker was put to death. The chief butler rejoiced in his good fortune, but he thought no more of Joseph.

Question 6 ❖ Whose dreams did Joseph interpret?

Question 7 ❖ Did the chief butler remember to ask Pharaoh to release Joseph from prison?"

The Saints

Saint Patrick

Saint Patrick was born around 387. When he was sixteen, he was captured by pirates and sold as a slave to a master in Ireland. While looking after sheep in the mountains, he prayed constantly. After about six years he heard a voice from heaven telling him to go back to his own country. First he went to Rome where he became a priest. He was then sent to England where he worked for the Church for many years. However, he wanted to return to Ireland and he begged the Pope to send him there.

The Pope made him a bishop and then sent him as a missionary to Ireland. One of the pagan kings of Ireland arrested Patrick. When he saw the miracles worked by Patrick, he said, "Tell us about your God. He has given you great power. There is but one God," answered Patrick "and three Divine Persons, the Father, the Son and the Holy Ghost." Picking up a green shamrock he said, "Even as there are three leaves on this one stem, so there are three Persons in the one God."

The King allowed Saint Patrick to preach the new Faith every-where in Ireland.

Saint Patrick is the Patron Saint of Ireland and his feast day is 17th March.

Question 8 ❖ What did Saint Patrick use to explain the Blessed Trinity?

_____

Question 9 ❖ Which country is Saint Patrick the Patron?

_____

Question 10 ❖ Was Saint Patrick a Bishop or a Pope?

_____

The Rosary

The Rosary calls to mind the most important events in the lives of Jesus and Mary. These events are called Mysteries, there are 15 Mysteries in all. They are divided into three groups or decades.

> They are: The Joyful Mysteries
> The Sorrowful Mysteries
> The Glorious Mysteries

How to Say the Rosary

1. Begin at the crucifix and say the Apostles' Creed.

2. On the first bead, say one Our Father.

3. On the next three beads, say three Hail Marys.

4. Next, say one Glory Be. Then announce and think of the first Mystery and say one Our Father.

5. Say ten Hail Marys, one Glory Be and the Fatima Prayer.

6. Announce the second Mystery and continue in the same way until each of the five Mysteries of the selected decades are said.

7. After the five decades are said, say the Hail Holy Queen and then finish with the Sign of the Cross.

Question 11 ❖ What are the three types of Mysteries in the Rosary ?

_____

_____

_____

Level 2 - Lesson 2

The Rosary

Question 12 ❖ How many Hail Marys are there in one decade?

Question 13 ❖ When holding the crucifix, what is the first prayer said in the Rosary?

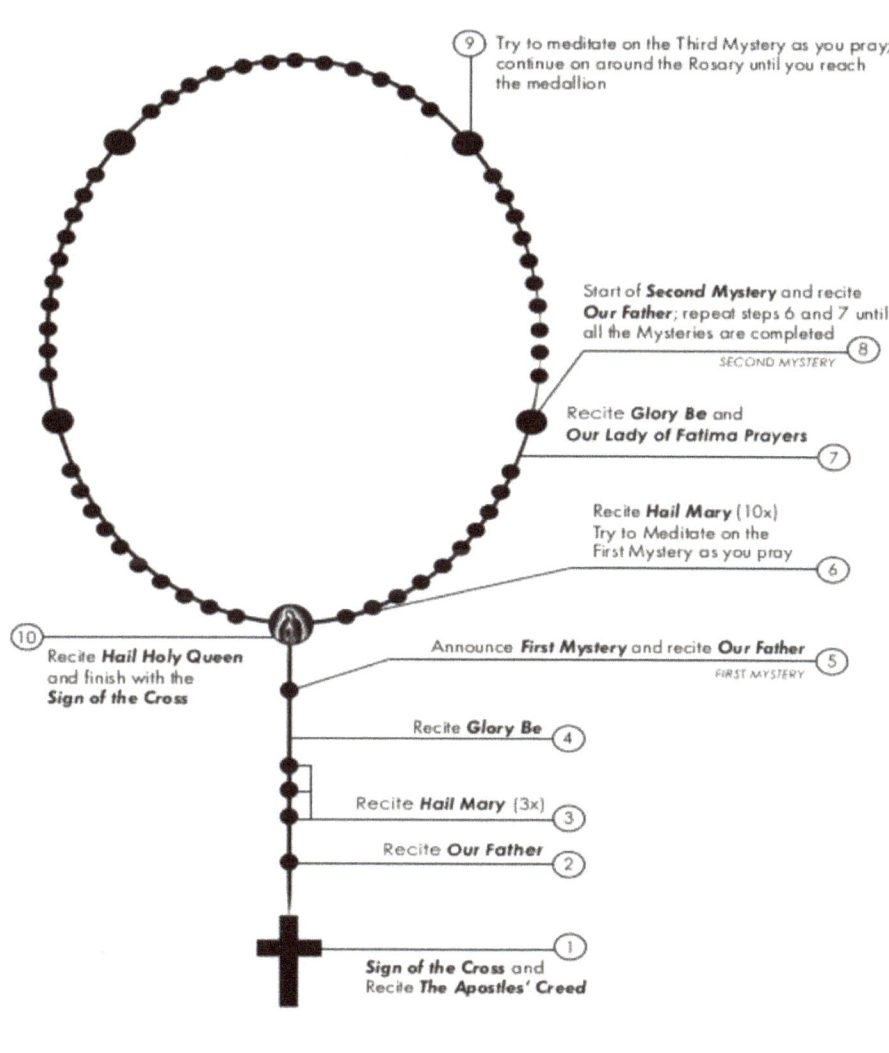

General

The Chasuble

The long, black garment that the priest wears is called a Cassock or Soutane. The word Cassock comes from the Italian word *"casacca"*, which means a great coat.

The cassock, or soutane is a garment reaching to the heals, and fastened down the front either with many small buttons, or hidden buttons (sometimes even a hidden zip).

It is the Ecclesiastical (Church) uniform of all priests and clerics, except those who belong to a Religious Order who wear a distinctive habit (for example, the Franciscans wear a brown habit).

The cassock of the Pope is WHITE

Cardinals wear RED

Bishops use PURPLE

Priests and Seminarians are in BLACK

Question 14 ❖ What is another name for the cassock ?

_____

Question 15 ❖ What does the Italian word for Cassock mean?

_____

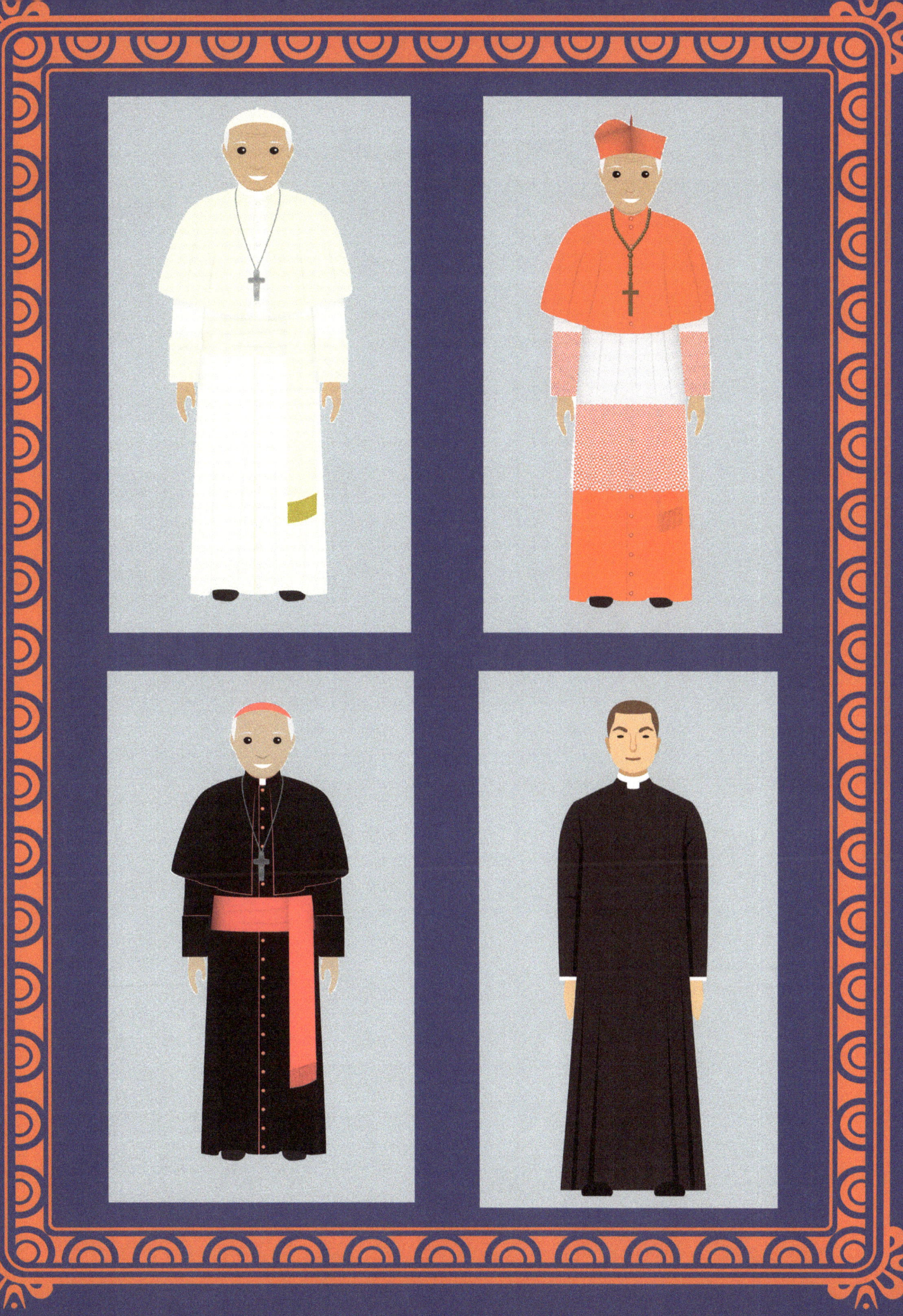

Lesson 3

Level 2

Post Communion Level

Catechism

God and His Perfections

8. **What do we mean when we say that God is the Supreme Being?**

   When we say that God is the Supreme Being we mean that He is above all creatures.

9. **What do we mean when we say that God is eternal?**

   When we say that God is eternal we mean that He always was and always will be, and that He always remains the same.

10. **What do we mean when we say that God is all-knowing?**

    When we say that God is all-knowing, we mean that He knows all things, past, present, and future, even our most secret thoughts, words and actions.

If we are to love and serve God as we should, we must first know about Him; that is why we are learning the catechism. In this lesson we are learning about God, as the Supreme Being; that means that in all ways, He is greater than us. That is because He is God. God had no beginning and has no end. God knows all things. He even knows what you are thinking right now as you read this lesson.
Let us always remember that God is the Supreme Being and we are His creatures, and creatures should always obey their Creator.

Question 1 ❖ What do we mean when we say God is eternal?

_____

Question 2 ❖ What do we mean when we say that God is the supreme being?

_____

Question 3 ❖ Where do we find the chief truths taught by Jesus Christ through the Catholic Church?

_____

Level 2 - Lesson 3

Prayer

The Decade Prayer

**O My Jesus, forgive us our sins,
save us from the fires of hell.
Lead all souls to heaven,
especially those who most need
Thy mercy.**

Almost a hundred years ago, about a year before Mary appeared to the three children, an angel appeared to them and taught them some prayers. Among these prayers was the Decade Prayer. The angel asked that this prayer be said at the end of each decade of the Rosary (after the Glory Be). If you do not already know it, learn it well and pray it every day when you pray with your family the Rosary.

Remember, whenever you pray, always think about the words you are saying. In this prayer, you are asking Jesus to save you from Hell and to help other souls to get to heaven.

Question 4 ❖ When do we pray the Decade prayer ?

Question 5 ❖ Who taught the three children the Decade Prayer?

Question 6 ❖ When should we say Grace before Meals?

Bible Story

Pharaoh's Dream

After two years, Pharaoh had a dream. He dreamt that he was standing by the river Nile and up came out of the water seven cows, very beautiful and fat. After them came also seven other cows, that were skinny and sickly, and they ate the fat ones, then the Pharaoh awoke.

Again the next night he slept he had another dream, this time he was dreaming that there were seven fields of corn, big healthy corns ready for harvest. The next dream the fields were full of thin rotten corn which overtook the fields of the beautiful corn.

When morning came, he sent for all the wise men of Egypt, and told them his dreams. But no one was able to interpret them. Then the chief butler remembered Joseph, and said, "There is in prison a youth, who on one occasion interpreted dreams for me and for the chief baker, and all came true. So Pharaoh sent for Joseph and told him his two dreams. Joseph said, "The seven beautiful cows and the fields of corn are seven years of prosperity. But the seven skinny and sickly cows and the seven fields of rotten corn are seven years of famine. Joseph told the Pharaoh to choose a wise man who shall store up in barns enough food for seven years so that it be ready when the seven years of famine begin.

This advice was pleasing to Pharaoh, and he said to Joseph, "Can I find such a man that is full of the spirit of God? You shall be in charge of my house, and at your commandment all the people shall obey."

Pharaoh then took the ring from his own hand, and placed it on Joseph's hand. He also put on him a robe of silk, and placed a chain of gold around his neck. Then he instructed Joseph to be seated in a triumphal chariot, and a he cried out, "Bend your knees to Joseph, for he is the governor of the whole land of Egypt."

Question 7 ❖ Who interpreted Pharaoh's dreams?

_____

Question 8 ❖ Was Pharaoh pleased with Joseph's interpretation of his dreams?

_____

Question 9 ❖ What position of importance did Pharaoh give Joseph?

_____

Question 10 ❖ Where did the merchants take Joseph?

_____

The Saints

Saint Christopher

The word "Christopher" means Christ Bearer. Lets read the story of Saint Christopher and we will see why his name means Christ Bearer.

Saint Christopher was a very large and strong man. He was a pagan, who was later converted to Christianity by a holy hermit, who told him that he should dedicate his life to the heavenly King. Saint Christopher built a hut along a dangerous stream, where many drowned trying to cross it, he helped many people across.

One day, a little child came to Saint Christopher and he lifted up the boy onto his shoulder, as he crossed the river the child was becoming heavier and heavier. On reaching the other side, and putting the child down, Saint Christopher said, "Child, you put me in dire peril; you weighed so heavy I felt as if I was carrying the whole world on my shoulders."

The boy replied, "Do not wonder that you have carried the whole world on your shoulders, but also He who created the world." Saint Christopher had actually carried the Child Jesus across the stream, his name truly means, Christ Bearer.

Saint Christopher is the Patron Saint of travelers. Many people keep a Saint Christopher medal in their car, and have one with them where ever they travel.

Saint Christopher's feast day is July 25th.

Question 11 ❖ Who did Saint Christopher carry on his shoulders?
_____

Question 12 ❖ Who is Saint Christopher the patron of?
_____

Question 13 ❖ What Religious Order did Saint John Bosco found?
_____

Question 14 ❖ What did Saint Patrick use to explain the Blessed Trinity?
_____

The Rosary

When we pray the ten Hail Marys, we should be meditating (thinking) about the mysteries. Read carefully what is written about each Mystery and think about these things when praying the Rosary.

The First Joyful Mystery - The Annunciation

While Mary was at prayer, God sent the Angel Gabriel to her. He said, "Hail, full of grace, the Lord is with thee". He then told her she was to become the Mother of Jesus; the Mother of God. With humility, and with her eyes looking down, Our Blessed Lady asked the angel "how this could be?".

The Angel Gabriel explained that it would be done by the power of the Holy Ghost.

Our Lady answered: "Be it done unto me according to thy word." And at that moment the Incarnation took place.

Let us learn to imitate Mary's humility. We often want to show others how good we are at our school work or at sport. Let us ask Our Lady for the wonderful gift of humility. This is something we can ask for when we pray the First Joyful Mystery. We ask God during this mystery to give us the spirit of humility.

The Second Joyful Mystery - The Visitation

Soon afterwards, Mary went to visit her cousin Saint Elizabeth who was soon to have a baby (Saint John the Baptist). She spent three months helping Saint Elizabeth with all the house work and other chores. What an example Our Lady is to us.

When we pray this Mystery let us ask for the gift of charity. No one was ever more charitable than Mary. If we pray and ask for this grace, she will surely give it to us. We ask God during this mystery that we might be more charitable to our neighbor.

Level 2 - Lesson 3

General

The Biretta

The special cap worn by the priest is called a Biretta (Italian word for cap). It used to be a soft, round cap. Later three ridges or peaks were added, so that it could be taken off and put on more easily. These three peaks represent the Blessed Trinity.

The Biretta is worn by all clerics (seminarians, priests, bishops, cardinals) on entering and leaving the church and during ceremonies. Some well known Saints such as Saint John Bosco used to wear his Biretta often.

Cardinals wear red birettas, bishops wear purple, and priests and seminarians wear black.

Question 15 ❖ What do the three peak on the Biretta represent?

___

Question 16 ❖ What color Biretta does a priest wear?

___

Question 17 ❖ When does a priest wear a Biretta?

___

Question 18 ❖ Why does a Biretta have ridges/peaks?

___

Lesson 4

Level 2

Post Communion Level

Catechism

God and His Perfections

11. **What do we mean when we say God is all-present?**

    When we say that God is all-present we mean that He is everywhere.

12. **Does God see us?**

    God sees us and watches over us with loving care.

13. **What do we mean when we say that God is almighty?**

    When we say that God is almighty we mean that He can do all things.

Yes, God is the Supreme Being, He is eternal, He is all-knowing, He is all-present, He sees us and He is almighty. These are the perfections of God. Learn these catechism questions well and with the help of your parent and teacher, try to understand as best you can what these catechism questions and answers mean.

We cannot hide from God. He sees all we do, all we say and even all we think. He is everywhere and is looking over us and protecting us so that we might one day be with Him in heaven.

Question 1 ❖ Does God see us ?

_____

Question 2 ❖ What do we mean when we say God is all-present ?

_____

Question 3 ❖ What do we mean when we say that God is the Supreme Being?

_____

Prayer

Level 2 - Lesson 4

In this Lesson we are going to revise a prayer we learnt in Level One, the Act of Contrition. Every night before we go to bed, we should make an examination of our conscience. That is, we should think about all the things we have done throughout the day and see if we have offended God by sinning. After we have thought about our sins, we then tell God we are sorry by praying the Act of Contrition.

**O my God I am sorry and beg pardon for all my sins. I detest them above all things because they deserve Thy dreadful punishments, because they have crucified my loving Saviour Jesus Christ and most of all because they offend Thy Infinite Majesty. I firmly resolve by the help of Thy grace never to offend Thee again and carefully to avoid the occasions of sin.
Amen**

Question 4

Why is the longer Act of Contrition better to say in Confession than the shorter Act of Contrition?

_____

Question 4 ❖ Write out the Decade Prayer :

_____

_____

_____

_____

Bible Story

The Famine

Nine years after Joseph had been sold, there came a terrible famine, and Jacob (Joseph's father) sent ten of his sons to Egypt to buy corn. Benjamin, his youngest son stayed at home, as he feared that something would happen to him..

Joseph was in charge of the corn in Egypt, and when his brothers came to him he knew them at once, though they did not know him. He pretended to take them for spies, and cast Simeon, one of the eldest, into prison. Then he told the others to go home to their father with the corn they had bought, promising to free Simeon if they would come back with their youngest brother, Benjamin.

The brothers felt that God was now punishing them for their wickedness, and went off quite sad. When they reached home they told everything to their father. At first Jacob refused to let Benjamin go, but when the corn was all eaten up, he was obliged to consent.
The brothers soon reached Egypt and were at once taken to Joseph's palace. Joseph wept for joy when he saw Benjamin, and blessed the boy. He asked his brothers to dine with him, and set them at the table in the order of their age. The next morning their sacks were filled with corn, and they started their journey home. They had not gone far, when a servant came hurrying after them, accusing one of them of stealing a silver cup.

To prove that they had not done such a wicked thing, they went back; but when they were searched, the missing cup was found, hidden in Benjamin's sack

Joseph had secretly ordered one of his servants to hide the cup in his brothers sack, to test them. When they saw it, they fell at Joseph's feet, and offered to be his slaves. He let them all go home except Benjamin, who stayed to be his slave.

At this, Juda, one of the brothers, begged Joseph to keep him for a slave, and let Benjamin go, saying that their dear old father would die of grief if Benjamin did not return.

Joseph knew by this, that his brothers were no longer the bad men they used to be. All the strangers were ordered to leave the room, and when they were alone, Joseph said: "I am Joseph, your brother. Be not afraid, for God sent me to Egypt that you might have food, when you needed it."

Then he embraced Benjamin and his other brothers, gave them many presents, and sent them home to their father.
.

Level 2 - Lesson 4

Bible Story

As soon as Jacob heard that his beloved son was still alive, he prepared to go to Egypt, taking with him his whole family. Joseph hastened to meet him, and seeing him, fell on his neck, weeping.

"Now shall I die with joy," said Jacob, "because I have seen thy face." Almost these same words were used, seventeen hundred years afterwards, by the holy Simeon, when he saw our divine Saviour presented as a babe in the Temple.

Joseph gave his father and his brothers land on which to feed their flocks, and they became a great nation.

Seventeen years after his arrival in Egypt Jacob died, but Joseph lived to be a hundred and ten years old; and saw his great grand-children before his death.

Joseph's life was, in many ways, a picture of the life of Our Saviour Jesus. Joseph was hated by his brothers because of his goodness; Jesus too was hated. Joseph was betrayed and sold; so was Jesus. Joseph triumphed in the end, and was made governor of Egypt; Jesus was victorious over death, and is King of Heaven and of earth. Joseph saved his brothers from dying by famine; Jesus Christ died to save us from the death of sin.

Question 5 ❖ Why did Jacob keep Benjamin at Home ?

_____

Question 6 ❖ Into whose sack did Joseph place the cup ?

_____

Question 7 ❖ Was Joseph happy to see Benjamin ?

_____

Question 8 ❖ Joseph's life was, in many ways a picture of Whose life ?

_____

The Saints

Saint John Vianney (The Cure of Ars)

All priests, when they are ordained, are given a very special power by God to forgive sins in the Sacrament of Penance. A few holy priests have had a very special gift of reconciling sinners to God – that is, making sinners friends again with God. Saint John Vianney was one of these priests. He was holy and famous as a Confessor. He is the Patron Saint of parish priests.

Saint John Vianney was born of a poor French family in 1786. This was just before the beginning of the French Revolution, which caused great difficulties for Catholics, even in being able to attend Mass. Churches were closed and priests killed. People met in secret for Mass.

A parish priest friend helped John with his early studies. He found study very hard. He was a slow learner. He was not ordained until he was nearly 30 years old, and then more because of his holiness than for being a clever student. His priestly life was spent in Ars, a small parish in France. He was a very holy priest. People came hundreds of miles to his little church, especially to go to Confession to the Cure (parish priest) of Ars.

People would line up for days just to go to him for confession. Many days, he would spend thirteen to seventeen hours just hearing confessions. God had given him the remarkable gift of seeing into people's hearts and souls – he knew their sins before they told him. He felt a very big sorrow for sinners. He felt sad for sinners who turned away from God. They did not want to know, love or serve God. He knew these sinners would go to hell if they didn't seek God's forgiveness.

Through many prayers and sacrifices, and the intercession of Saint Philomena, a saint in whom he had great confidence and whom he loved very much, he saved many souls for God. Saint John Vianney died in 1859.

His feast day is on August 8th.

Question 9 ❖ What was Saint John Vianney famous for ?

Question 10 ❖ Saint John Vianney was also known as ?

Question 11 ❖ Who was his special *helper* saint ?

The Rosary

When we pray the ten Hail Marys, we should be meditating (thinking) about the mysteries. Read carefully what is written about each Mystery and think about these things when praying the Rosary.

The Third Joyful Mystery - The Birth of Jesus

During this decade, as we pray the ten Hail Marys, we meditate (think) about the baby Jesus lying on the straw in the stable with Mary and Saint Joseph watching over him. We can also think of the angels coming to the shepherds singing, Glory to God in the highest and then the shepherds leaving their sheep to visit Jesus. We can even meditate about the visit of the Three Wise Men who came from afar to give their gifts to Jesus.

This Mystery of the Rosary is so rich in what we can meditate about. We ask God during this mystery to give us a spirit of poverty.

Question 12 ❖ What is one thing we can meditate on during this mystery?

Question 13 ❖ What gift do we ask of God during this mystery?

Question 14 ❖ How many Mysteries of the Rosary are there altogether?

Level 2 - Lesson 4

General

The Communion Plate

During Mass, the priest changes the bread and wine into the Body and Blood of Jesus, it is a miracle! During most Masses, the faithful receive Holy Communion.

When the priest gives Holy Communion to the people, the Altar Server holds a plate under the chin of the person so that no small particle of the Sacred Host will fall to the ground (the priest places the Sacred Host upon the tongue).

If there is no Altar Server, the person receiving Holy Communion must hold the plate himself, he must be careful to hold it straight, so that no particles drop on the ground.
A Communion Plate must always be used because Our Lord Himself is truly present in every little particle of the consecrated Host.

Another point to remember, is that Communion is always to be received on the tongue. The priest can touch the Sacred Host because his hands are especially consecrated. We are not worthy to touch the Body of Our Lord.

Question 15 ❖ Who usually holds the Communion plate?

_____

Question 16 ❖ Why is it important that we use a Communion plate?

_____

Lesson 5

Level 2

Post Communion Level

Catechism

The Unity and Trinity of God

14. **Is there only one God?**

    Yes, there is only one God

15. **How many Persons are there in God?**

    In God, there are three Divine Persons – the Father, the Son and the Holy Ghost

16. **What do we mean by the Blessed Trinity?**

    By the Blessed Trinity we mean one and the same God in three Divine Persons.

There are three Persons in the one God. This is a mystery of our Faith.
One day, hundreds of years ago, the great Saint Augustine was walking along the beach trying to fully understand the Mystery of the Blessed Trinity, when he came upon a young boy carrying a handful of sea water and putting it into a hole he had dug on the beach. This prompted Saint Augustine to ask the boy what he was doing. The boy replied, "I am going to take all the water from the ocean and put it in this hole I have dug". "That is impossible" said the Saint.
"But it is no more possible for you to fully understand the Blessed Trinity than for me to fill this hole with the whole ocean."
Saint Augustine understood the message from the little boy (who was actually an angel). He understood that the Mystery of the Blessed Trinity was a Mystery, and we will never understand it while on this earth. We cannot understand the Mystery of the Blessed Trinity. God simply asks us to believe it; to have faith.

Question 1 ❖ How many Persons are there in God ?

_____

Question 2 ❖ From whom do we learn to know, love and serve God ?

_____

Prayer

The Angelus

V. The angel of the Lord declared unto Mary
R. *And she conceived of the Holy Ghost*
Say the Hail Mary…
V. Behold the Handmaid of the Lord
R. *Be it done unto me according to thy word*
  Say the Hail Mary…
V. And the Word was made flesh
R. *And dwelt among us*
  Say the Hail Mary…
V. Pray for us O holy Mother of God
R. *That we may be made worthy of the promises of Christ*
V. Let us Pray

**Pour forth, we beseech Thee O Lord, Thy grace into our hearts, that we to whom the Incarnation of Christ, Thy Son was made known by the message of an angel, may by His Passion and Cross be brought to the glory of His resurrection, through the same Christ Our Lord.
   Amen.**

One of the very old Catholic customs is the saying of the "Angelus" prayer which is said three times each day. At sunrise (6:00am), midday (12:00noon) and sunset (6:00pm).
Whether mothers were cleaning the house, fathers were working in the fields, or the children were minding the sheep, everyone would stop what they were doing at the sound of the bell and say reverently the "Angelus" prayer. It is a wonderful tradition
If you cannot say it at these exact times, say it as near as possible; whatever fits in with the family. You can also use a bell to ring at these times and it can become your Angelus Bell.

Question 3 ❖ How many times a day should the Angelus be said?

___

Question 4 ❖ At what times should the Angelus be said?

___

Bible Story

The Story of Moses (Part 1)

After the death of Joseph, the Hebrews, who were the descendants of Jacob, increased so very fast that the King of Egypt was afraid they would become too powerful. To prevent this, he ordered that they should do very hard work in the country, and as that might not be enough, he commanded that every baby boy should be drowned as soon as he was born.

About this time, a Hebrew woman had a little boy whom she loved dearly. She wished to save her baby and so for three months she hid him. When she could hide him no longer, she made a basket of rushes which she daubed over with slime and pitch, so that the water could not enter, and with her heart almost breaking, she put her baby in it, and laid it in the high reeds, along the river's side. The baby's sister, whose name was Mary, hid near-by to watch.

Shortly after, the king's daughter came down to bathe at the river and seeing the basket, she called her servant. The princess opened it and saw a pretty little boy, and her heart was filled with pity for his poor mother. She made up her mind to save the child and raise him up as her son. The babies sister seeing this ran up to her and asked if she could find a nurse for him; being told to do so, she brought his mother. The baby was named Moses, which means saved from the water.

When Moses was forty years old, he set to work to help his countrymen, who were suffering many hardships. This displeased the king, who ordered Moses to be put to death; but he fled from Egypt to Madian in Arabia, where he became a shepherd.

One day, while Moses was watching his sheep, God appeared to him in a burning bush. Moses was surprised to see that the bush did not burn up, he went nearer to look at it. God commanded him to stand still and to take off his shoes, as the place was holy. At the voice of God, Moses fell on his face. Then God told him that he was chosen to free the Hebrews, and for this he must go before the King; and to take his brother Aaron to speak for him.

Question 5 ❖ Who was put into a basket and floated on the river that he might be saved from Pharaoh?

_____

Question 6 ❖ How did God appear to Moses?

_____

Question 7 ❖ What did God tell Moses?

_____

Question 8 ❖ Who was the spokesman for Moses?

_____

The Saints

Saint Bernadette

Saint Bernadette's parents were very poor. They lived near Lourdes, in France. One day in 1858, while Bernadette was collecting firewood, a beautiful Lady stood before her in a cave. She was dressed in blue and white and there were roses at her feet. She smiled at Bernadette and asked her to pray the Rosary with her.

Bernadette saw the Lady eighteen times. One time, the Lady said to Bernadette "I do not promise to make you happy in this world, but in the next."

Large crowds followed Bernadette to the grotto (cave) to pray the Rosary with her. They could not see the Lady. The Lady asked Bernadette to dig the earth and water began to flow miraculously from the ground. Many pilgrims, even to this day have been cured from the water.

When Bernadette asked the Lady her name, the Lady said I am the Immaculate Conception. Her message was to pray for sinners. She asked Bernadette that a church be built near the grotto. Today, there is a great Shrine to the Blessed Virgin Mary.

Later, Bernadette became a nun. She died at the age of thirty-six and her body is incorrupt. This means, that even though she died over 120 years ago, her body looks just like it did when she was alive, she still looks like she is sleeping.

Her feast day is February, 18th.

Question 9 ❖ What was the name that Our Lady called herself?
_____

Question 10 ❖ Where did Mary appear to Saint Bernadette?
_____

The Rosary

When we pray the ten Hail Marys, we should be meditating (thinking) about the mysteries. Read carefully what is written about each Mystery and think about these things when praying the Rosary.

The Fourth Joyful Mystery
The Presentation of Jesus in the Temple

In this Mystery we think about Mary and Saint Joseph taking the Baby Jesus to the Temple to present Him to God (the Father). We also remember that there were two holy people, Simeon and Anna, who were waiting for the coming of the Saviour. In fact, Simeon took Jesus into his arms, made a prophesy, and then said, "Now, Lord, You can dismiss Your servant in peace, for my eyes have seen Your Salvation".

Following the example of Our Lady and Saint Joseph we pray in this Mystery for the grace to be obedient to the Church and to God's Will.

The Fifth Joyful Mystery
The Finding in the Temple

In this Mystery, we contemplate when Jesus was lost for three days and how hard Mary and Saint Joseph searched for Him. We also think about the words Jesus said to his parents, "I must be about My Father's business."

We learn from this Mystery that we must do God's Will always, even when it is difficult or others think we are foolish. Remember what Saint Paul said, "We must be fools for Christ's sake."

Question 11 ❖ Who are the two holy people waiting for Jesus in the Temple?

_____

Question 12 ❖ For how long was Jesus lost?

_____

Level 2 - Lesson 5

General

The Altar

Things we see on the Altar

1 : Crucifix
2 : Canopy
3 : Tabernacle
4 : Altar cards
5 : Candlesticks
6 : Altar table
7 : Altar Cloths
8 : Altar Steps

Lesson 6

Level 2

Post Communion Level

Catechism

Creation and the Angels

17. **What do we mean when we say that God is the Creator of heaven and earth?**

    When we say that God is the Creator of heaven and earth we mean that He made all things from nothing.

18. **Which are the chief creatures of God?**

    The chief creatures of God are angels and men.

19. **What are angels?**

    Angels are created spirits without bodies.

20. **Did all the angels remain faithful to God?**

    Not all the angels remained faithful to God; some of them sinned.

God created everything! From the smallest grain of sand to the angels and saints. God also made the plants and the animals. God made all things for us so that we might love and serve Him and one day be with Him forever in heaven.

Question 1 ❖ What do we mean when we say that God is the Creator of heaven and earth?

_____

Question 2 ❖ How many Persons are there in God?

_____

Question 3 ❖ What do we mean by the Blessed Trinity?

_____

Prayer

Level 2 - Lesson 6

The Regina Coeli

V. **Queen of heaven, rejoice, Alleluia**
R. *For He Whom thou didst merit to bear, Alleluia*

V. **Hath risen as He said, Alleluia**
R. *Pray for us to God, Alleluia*

V. **Rejoice and be glad O Virgin Mary, Alleluia**
R. *For the Lord is truly risen, Alleluia*

V. **Let us Pray:**

O God, Who by the resurrection of Thy Son, Our Lord Jesus Christ, hast vouchsafed to make glad the whole world, grant we beseech Thee, that through the intercession of the Virgin Mary His Mother, we may attain the joys of eternal life. Through the same Christ Our Lord. Amen.

During the Easter season, the Church replaces the "Angelus" prayer with the "Regina Coeli" prayer to remind us of the great Mystery of the Resurrection of Our Lord Jesus Christ. Like the Angelus, the prayer is said morning, noon and evening.

Question 4 ❖ How many times a day should the Regina Coeli be said?

_____

Question 5 ❖ Write out Grace Before Meals

_____

_____

_____

Bible Story

The Story of Moses (Part 2)

Moses and Aaron went to the Egyptian king and told him that God had ordered him to free the Hebrews. The king not only refused to do this, but even gave the people harder work than before. Moses and Aaron went again to the king, who refused a second time to do as he was told. For his disobedience God sent ten plagues on the Egyptian king and his people.

At first, the water of the rivers was changed to blood; then frogs covered the whole country; after that the dust of the earth turned into small insects which troubled both men and beasts; next came a plague of flies which filled all the houses; and then a disease which killed the cattle. The sixth plague was boils on men and animals; the seventh plague a hail-storm which destroyed the grain and fruits; the eighth, a plague of locusts to eat what the hail had spared; and the ninth a dreadful darkness for three long days.

Before sending the tenth and most terrible plague, God ordered each Hebrew family to sacrifice a lamb on the fourteenth day of the month, and to sprinkle the doorposts of each house with its blood; then to roast the lamb and eat its flesh with unleavened bread: all of which was done.

That night God's angel visited the houses that were not marked with the blood of the lamb and there was great mourning among the Egyptians; for in every home from that of the king down to the poorest man, the eldest child lay dead. Then the king sent for Moses and Aaron and freed the Hebrews telling them to leave Egypt. Moses at once gathered all his people, but after a few days, the king regretted letting them go, wanting to seek vengeance he and his army went after them. When the Hebrews, who were on the shores of the Red Sea saw the army coming, they were frightened as there was only the sea in front of them with nowhere to escape. But Moses told them to not fear and stretching forth his rod over the sea, as God commanded him, the waters of the sea divided, rising like a wall to the right and the left, leaving a dry passage through which the people crossed over to the other side.

When Moses reached the other side he saw the Egyptians following, Moses again stretched his rod over the sea and the waters rolled back to their place, and the king with his whole army drowned. This passage through the Red Sea is a figure of Holy Baptism, by which we are freed from the slavery of sin.

Question 6 ❖ How many plagues did God send upon the Egyptians?

_____

Question 7 ❖ What was the last plague God sent the Egyptians?

_____

Question 8 ❖ Who was put into a basket and floated on the river so that he might be saved from Pharaoh?

_____

The Saints

Saint Veronica

When Jesus was carrying His heavy Cross to Calvary, where the Roman soldiers were going to crucify Him, a lady who was watching touched by grace, wanted to help Jesus and relieve Him of some of His sufferings. This lady is Saint Veronica. She did not think of herself nor of what others would think of her as she was motivated only by a love for Our Blessed Lord.

She bravely went to Jesus and gave Him her veil that He might wipe His Face which was covered with blood from the terrible treatment He had received. As a reward for Saint Veronica's charity, Our Lord left an image of His Sacred Face on the veil which Saint Veronica treasured for the remainder of her life. . Let us ask Saint Veronica for the grace to love Our dear Saviour above all things and let us imitate her by comforting Our Lord with our prayers and sacrifices.

Saint Veronica's feast day is on July 9th

Question 9 ❖ What did Saint Veronica do to try to help Jesus as He was on the way to Calvary?

_____

Question 10 ❖ Where did Mary appear to Saint Bernadette?

_____

The Rosary

The First Sorrowful Mystery ; The Agony in the Garden
After the Last Supper, Jesus took His Apostles to the Garden of Olives that He might pray and prepare Himself for His Passion and death on the Cross. He asked His apostles to pray, but they fell asleep. In fact, He asked them three times to pray and three times they fell asleep.
Jesus prayed to His Heavenly Father, and although Jesus in His human nature feared his upcoming suffering, He said to His Father, "Not My Will, but yours be done".
This mystery teaches us that we should pray often and well, and that we should always strive to do God's Will, not our own.

The Second Sorrowful Mystery ; The Scourging at the Pillar
After praying in the Garden, Jesus was taken to the High Priest who ordered Jesus to be taken to Pilate to be crucified. Pilate saw that Jesus was guilty of no crime, but had Him scourged anyway. How unjust! While Jesus was being scourged, He never complained. He did not complain about His unjust sentence, nor about the terrible suffering the scourging was causing Him. He offered all His sufferings for us. In this Mystery, we ask Our Blessed Lord to give us the grace not to complain about our sufferings and that we might offer our sufferings up for those who need them.

Question 11 ❖ How many times did the Apostles fall asleep?

Question 12 ❖ To whom did Jesus pray in the Garden?

Question 13 ❖ Did Pilate find Jesus innocent or guilty?

Question 14 ❖ How many mysteries of the Rosary are there altogether?

Question 15 ❖ What is the Third Joyful Mystery?

Level 2 - Lesson 6

General

The Tabernacle

The Tabernacle is like a little house and should be placed in the most prominent part of the Church, which is at the middle of the Altar.

It is usually made of brass, strong wood or marble. It is very important that it is strong and can be securely locked. This is the place where the consecrated hosts are kept; this is Our Lord's special home where He can be loved and adored.

A lighted sanctuary lamp and a veil on the Tabernacle are the two signs that Our Blessed Lord is present in the Tabernacle.

When we enter a church, we look at the Tabernacle and genuflect because Our Lord is there.

Sometimes we go into a church and pray to Our Lord in the Tabernacle.

Our Lord likes us to visit Him in the church whenever we can.

Question 16 ❖ What is a Tabernacle?

_____

Question 17 ❖ What is kept in the Tabernacle?

_____

Lesson 7

Level 2

Post Communion Level

Catechism

Creation and the Angels

21. **What happened to the angels who remained faithful to God?**

The angels who remained faithful to God entered into the eternal happiness of heaven, and these are called good angels.

22. **How do the good angels help us?**

The good angels help us by praying for us, by acting as messengers from God to us, and by serving as our guardian angels.

23. **What happened to the angels who did not remain faithful to God?**

The angels who did not remain faithful to God were cast into hell, and these are called bad angels or devils.

Before God created us, He created the angels. Angels are pure spirits, who, having passed the test God gave them and are eternally happy with Him in heaven. The angels who rebelled against God were cast into hell and are now devils.

God has given each one of us our own special angel, our Guardian Angel, who looks over us and protects us. We should pray to our guardian angel each day and he will help us fight temptation and love God better.

Question 1 ❖ What happened to the Angels who remained faithful to God?

_____

Question 2 ❖ What are angels?

_____

Level 2 - Lesson 7

Prayer

The Apostles Creed

In this lesson we are going to revise The Apostles' Creed. It is important to know this prayer by heart and to understand the best we can, the truths it teaches. This prayer covers the most important teachings of God's holy Church.

I believe in God, the Father Almighty, Creator of heaven and earth; and in Jesus Christ, His only Son, Our Lord; Who was conceived by the Holy Ghost, born of the Virgin Mary, suffered under Pontius Pilate, was crucified, died and was buried. He descended into hell; the third day He arose again from the dead; He ascended into heaven, sitteth at the right hand of God, the Father Almighty, from thence He shall come to judge the living and the dead. I believe in the Holy Ghost, the Holy Catholic Church, the communion of saints, the forgiveness of sins, the resurrection of the body, and life everlasting. Amen.

Question 3 ❖ Using the Apostles creed, list 3 things we must believe in as Catholics ?

_____

_____

_____

Bible Story

The Story of Moses (Part 3)

The Quails, the Manna, and the Water in the Desert

When the Hebrews had crossed the Red Sea they came into a desert, and soon their food was all gone. They could find nothing to eat; but God in His goodness, sent a number of quails into their camp, and caused a fine bread, called manna, to fall from heaven. Later on, when they reached Mount Horeb and had no water, God ordered Moses to strike the rock with his rod, and water at once poured forth in great quantity. The manna which was sent down to feed the hungry Hebrews, or Israelites, as they were also called, was a figure of the Most Blessed Sacrament in which our Divine Lord gives Himself as food for our souls.

The Ten Commandments

Three months after leaving Egypt, the Israelites came to Mount Sinai. Here God called Moses up to the mountain, and commanded him to tell the people that if they remained faithful to the Lord, He would continue to protect them, and would make them a chosen people. God also commanded the people to prepare themselves for two whole days, so as to be ready for the third day. On the morning of the third day it began to thunder and lighten; a thick cloud covered the mountain, and the top of Mount Sinai seemed to be on fire. Then came the sound of a trumpet that grew louder and louder until the people trembled with fear. When Moses had led the people to the foot of the mountain, God spoke thus:

I. I am the Lord thy God. Thou shalt not have strange gods before me.

II. Thou shalt not take the name of the Lord thy God in vain.

III. Remember that thou keep holy the Sabbath-day.

IV. Honor thy father and thy mother.

V. Thou shalt not kill.

VI. Thou shalt not commit adultery.

VII. Thou shalt not steal.

VIII. Thou shalt not bear false witness against thy neighbor

IX. Thou shalt not covet thy neighbor's wife.

X. Thou shalt not covet thy neighbor's goods.

Level 2 - Lesson 7

Bible Story

The Israelites, who were trembling with fear, promised to do all that God commanded. Afterwards, Moses went up to the mountain again, and stayed there for forty days and forty nights, conversing with God, who gave him two stone tablets, on which were written the Ten Commandments.

Question 4 ❖ What were the two types of food God provided for the Israelites?

_____

Question 5 ❖ How many Commandments did God give to Moses?

_____

Question 6 ❖ On what mountain did God give the Commandments to Moses?

_____

The Saints

Saint Simon of Cyrene

Simon of Cyrene was a man standing near Jesus as He carried His heavy Cross along the road to Mount Calvary. The cruel soldiers looked at Jesus and not wanting Him to die before they could nail Him on the Cross, they ordered Simon to help Our Lord carry His sacred Cross.

Simon did not want to do this because the people would jeer at him, as he was not yet a follower of Jesus, but the soldiers forced him. But as soon as he held the Cross, his soul was flooded with graces and he felt completely different. He was a new man.

Simon then carried the Cross as if it were a wonderful privilege. He felt such a great joy in his heart knowing that he had been able to share in Our Lord's sufferings.

Imagine, if you can, that you are Saint Simon of Cyrene every single day and that you are helping Jesus to carry His heavy Cross, by your little acts of kindness, being cheerful when things go wrong, helping when you do not want to. Pray to Saint Simon to help you become a true friend of Our Lord Jesus Christ.

Question 7 ❖ At first, did Saint Simon want to help Jesus carry His cross ?

_____

Question 8 ❖ What made Saint Simon change his mind and want to help Our lord carry His Cross?

_____

The Rosary

When we pray the ten Hail Marys, we should be meditating (thinking) about the mysteries. Read carefully what is written about each Mystery and think about these things when praying the Rosary.

The Third Sorrowful Mystery ; The Crowning with Thorns
After Our Blessed Lord had been scourged at the Pillar, the soldiers mocked Him and made a crown of thorns for His Sacred Head. They forced the sharp crown onto Our Lord's Head and then pretended to adore Him as king. Oh, how sad it is to see people make fun of, or make jokes about Our Lord. He could easily have stopped this mockery, but He hung His Head and accepted all their sarcasm, their spitting and their hitting Him without even once complaining.
Let us ask Our Lord in this Mystery for the grace to accept all the bad things others say about us and to offer up all these hurts in reparation for our sins.

The Fourth Sorrowful Mystery ;The Carrying of the Cross
Jesus loves us so much that He allowed the soldiers to place on His shoulders a rough, heavy cross. He carried that cross all the way to Calvary, where they eventually put Him to death. Jesus gives each one of us a cross to carry, and asks us to carry it without complaining. To each of us He gives a different cross; to one it is poor health, to another poverty, to another it might be difficulty in learning. Whatever cross Jesus gives to us, let us embrace it and offer it up.
So while meditating on this Mystery, remember the Cross Our Blessed Lord carried all the way to Calvary, but remember also to accept the cross that Jesus gives you.

Question 9 ❖ What did the soldiers pretend to do when they crowned Jesus with thorns ?

Question 10 ❖ To where did Jesus carry His Cross?

Question 11 ❖ Does Jesus give everyone a cross to carry?

General

Holy Water

When you walk into a church, have you ever noticed that as you enter, there is some water just inside the doors? This is not just normal water; it is Holy Water and it is kept in a Holy Water Font.

Holy water is water that has been made special by a priest. The priest mixes salt to the water and gives it a special blessing and it becomes Holy Water, which is very powerful against the devil.

When we enter a church, we dip our fingers in the Holy Water Font and bless ourselves by making a Sign of the Cross. Holy Water is a Sacramental. That means that we should bless ourselves with it as often as we can because we will get special graces from God.

Many people also have a Holy Water Font inside the front door of their house, so that every time they go in or out of the house, they bless themselves. When they run out of Holy Water, they go to a priest and get some more. Have you got some Holy Water in your house?

Question 12 ❖ Where is Holy water usually kept ?

_____

Question 13 ❖ What makes Holy water different from Ordinary tap water?

_____

Question 14 ❖ What is kept in the Tabernacle?

_____

Question 15 ❖ Why is it important that we use a Communion Plate?

_____

Lesson 8

Level 2

Post Communion Level

Catechism

The Creation and the Fall of Man

24. **What is man?**

Man is a creature of God composed of body and soul, and made to the image and likeness of God.

25. **Who were the first man and woman?**

The first man and woman were Adam and Eve.

26. **What commandment did God give Adam and Eve?**

God gave Adam and Eve the commandment not to eat of the fruit of a certain tree that grew in the Garden of Paradise.

27. **Did Adam and Eve obey the Commandment of God?**

Adam and Eve did not obey the commandment of God, but ate of the forbidden fruit.

God made our first parents, Adam and Eve. They were the first man and woman. God made all things on the earth for Adam and Eve, for their children, and for all who would come after them. God gave Adam and Eve a choice, a test. They had to choose between what God wanted and what they wanted. Would it be God or themselves? Would they choose to serve God or to serve themselves?

Alas, they listened to the temptations of the devil and decided to disobey God.

Let us always love and obey God and do His Will, not our own selfish will.

Question 1 ❖ Did Adam and Eve obey the Commandment of God?

_____

Question 2 ❖ What are angels?

_____

Level 2 - Lesson 8

Prayer

Hail Holy Queen

In this lesson we are going to learn the Hail Holy Queen. It is a beautiful prayer to Our Blessed Mother that we can say at any time. But we most usually say this prayer at the end of the Rosary.

**Hail, Holy Queen, Mother of Mercy,
hail, our life, our sweetness and our hope!
To thee do we cry, poor banished children of Eve!
To thee do we send up our sighs,
mourning and weeping in this valley of tears.
Turn then, most gracious advocate,
thine eyes of mercy towards us;
and after this, our exile,
show unto us the blessed fruit of thy womb, Jesus.
O clement, O loving, O sweet Virgin Mary!**

Question 3 ❖ To whom are we praying when we pray the Hail Holy Queen?

_____

Question 4 ❖ When do we usually say the Hail Holy Queen?

_____

Bible Story

The Golden Calf

While Moses was staying on the mountain, the people began to complain, and going to Aaron, asked him to make them gods like those of the Egyptians. Thinking to quiet them, he told them to bring him the golden ear-rings and jewelery of their wives and daughters. To his great surprise, they did; so, being afraid to put them off any longer, Aaron made a golden calf of the ear-rings and jewelery, and gave it to the people to worship.

When Moses came down from the mountain and found the people adoring this idol, dancing about it and eating and drinking like pagans, he was so angry that he threw the stone tablets on which the Commandments were written, and they were broken in their fall. Taking the Golden Calf, he cast it into the fire, and ordered all who continued in idolatry to be put to death. Moses then returned once more to the mountain and begged God to pardon his people. The Lord heard his prayer, and Moses having made two stone tablets like the first, God wrote the Ten Commandments on them. When Moses came down from the mountain this time, his face shone so brightly that he was obliged to wear a veil, for the people dared not look upon him.

The Sin of Moses

The last year that the Israelites were in the desert, they camped at a place where there was no water. God told Moses to strike a rock once with his rod. Moses hesitated for a moment; then struck the rock two times, and water at once gushed forth. For his disobedience in striking the rock a second time God said that Moses should never enter the Promised Land.

The Death of Moses

The time had now come for Moses to die, so he called his people together, reminded them of all that God had done for them, ordered them to keep the Commandments, and named Josue as his successor.
When he had finished speaking he went up to the top of Mount Nebo, from which the Lord showed him Chanaan, the Promised Land. Full of faith and thanks to God for all his favors, Moses died at the age of one hundred and twenty years.

Level 2 - Lesson 8

Bible Story

Question 5 ❖ While Moses was on the mountain, who made the golden calf?

_____

Question 6 ❖ Why was Moses never allowed to enter the Promised Land?

_____

Question 7 ❖ How old was Moses when he died?

_____

Question 8 ❖ On what mountain did God give the Commandments to Moses?

_____

The Saints

Saint Thomas Aquinas

In this lesson we are going to learn about St Thomas Aquinas, one of the most intelligent and holiest men who has ever lived.

Thomas, the Count of Aquino (in Italy) left the University of Naples because he wanted to live with, and become a Dominican Priest. His two brothers brought him back and locked him in a castle for almost two years to keep him from returning to the monastery. The Pope wanted to talk with Thomas, so he called him to Rome.

The Pope commanded Thomas' mother and brothers not to try and stop him from becoming a priest. Thomas went back to the Dominicans, who sent him to study in France and Germany. Thomas became a priest and a great teacher. He wrote many books about the teachings of the Catholic Church. Known for his great love of Jesus in the Blessed Sacrament he wrote prayers and hymns which the Church uses today to honor the Holy Eucharist.

One day, as Thomas was praying before a large crucifix, Our Lord spoke to him: "Thomas, you have written well of Me. What do you want in return?" Thomas replied, "Lord, I want nothing else but Thee." He died at the age of forty seven in the year 1274. He is one of the greatest Saints of the Church and is called a Doctor of the Church. He is the Patron Saint of Catholic Schools, of Universities and Theologians.

Saint Thomas Aquinas feast day is on March 7th.

Question 9 ❖ Who did not want Thomas to become a priest?

_____

Question 10 ❖ What order did St Thomas join?

_____

Question 11 ❖ What made Saint Simon of Cyrene change his mind and want to help Our Lord carry His Cross?

_____

The Rosary

When we pray the ten Hail Marys, we should be meditating (thinking) about the mysteries. Read carefully what is written about each Mystery and think about these things when praying the Rosary.

The Fifth Sorrowful Mystery - The Crucifixion

The greatest day in the history of the world was the day that our Blessed Lord died on the Cross; the first Good Friday. Many people back then, and now think is was a day of defeat. But NO! It was the day that the gates of heaven were opened. After the terrible sin of Adam and Eve, no-one could get to heaven; the gates were closed!

But Jesus so loves us that He suffered and died for us. We remember the scourging, the crowning with thorns and the heavy cross He had to carry. How much He suffered! How much He loves us! In this mystery, let us imagine that we are standing at the foot of the Cross when Jesus said, "Father, forgive them, for they know not what they do." For Jesus was also talking about us when we sin.

Question 12 ❖ Why did Jesus die on the Cross?

_____

Question 13 ❖ What took place on the first Good Friday?

_____

General

Level 2 - Lesson 8

The Seven Corporal Works of Mercy

Saint James said that Faith without good works is dead. We must show God that we love Him by the way we love our neighbor. Over the next seven lessons we are going to study the Corporal Works of Mercy. Let us not only study them, but put them into practice, for such actions will surely help us get to heaven.

To Feed the Hungry

Although we cannot give great sums of money to charities or the missions that they might have enough food to feed themselves, we can help others around us when they are in need.

If someone at school has forgotten their lunch, we can share some of ours with them. This is a very charitable and heroic act, especially if we are hungry.

Perhaps, at times during the year, you can help mum and dad to go through the pantry and pack some good can foods and send them to someone in need. You may even have a friend whose family has little money. Your little acts of generosity will be rewarded very generously by God.

Jesus said in the Bible, "Whatsoever you do to the least of my brethren, you do unto Me". Whenever we show charity by feeding our neighbor, we are showing God Himself how much we love Him.

Question 14 ❖ What is the first Corporal Works of Mercy?

_____

Question 15 ❖ Which Saint said, "Faith without good works is dead?"

_____

Question 16 ❖ Why is it important that we use a Communion Plate?

_____

Lesson 9

Level 2

Post Communion Level

Catechism

The Creation and the Fall of Man

28. What happened to Adam and Eve on account of their sin?

On account of their sin Adam and Eve lost sanctifying grace and the right to heaven, and were driven from the Garden of Paradise.

29. What has happened to us on account of the sin of Adam?

On account of the sin of Adam we come into the world without grace, and we inherit his punishment.

30. What is this sin in us called?

This sin in us is called original sin.

31. Was any human person ever free from original sin?

The Blessed Virgin Mary was free from original sin, and this favor is called her Immaculate Conception.

Each one of us is born with Original Sin on our soul. We have inherited this sin from our first parents, Adam and Eve. We cannot attain heaven with this sin on our souls; that is why, as soon as possible after we are born, our parents take us to the church to have us baptized.

Once we are baptized, Original Sin is wiped from our souls and we become children of God. However, our souls are still weakened by Original Sin and we are still inclined to do evil. Our entire lives need to be a fight against our fallen nature, so that we may one day reach heaven.

Question 1 ❖ What happened to Adam and Eve on account of their sin?

_____

Question 2 ❖ Was any human person ever free from original sin?

_____

Level 2 - Lesson 9

Prayer

The Pardon Prayer

In this lesson we are going to learn the Pardon Prayer taught to the three children of Fatima by the Angel of Peace

My God,
I believe,
I adore,
I hope
and
I love You!

I beg pardon for those
who do not believe,
do not adore,
do not hope
and
do not love You!

Question 3 ❖ This prayer is a short act of Faith, Hope and what?

_____

Question 4 ❖ Who taught the three children the Pardon Prayer?

_____

Question 5 ❖ To whom are we praying when we pray the Hail Holy Queen?

_____

Bible Story

The Flight into Egypt

When Joseph went to sleep one night, an angel came to him, and said: "Arise, and take Mary and the Child into Egypt, and stay there until I tell you to return, for Herod has it in his mind to kill Jesus." Joseph called Mary, and told her, and they set out at once for Egypt.

When Herod found out that the Wise Men did not return he was furious, because he knew they had seen the Child, and would not tell him. He was a cruel, wicked man, and he told his soldiers to kill all the baby boys they could find in Bethlehem under two years of age. Just fancy how those mothers cried when the soldiers went up to them, and took the babies from their arms, and out of their beds, and killed them all. Herod hoped that the soldiers might find Jesus amongst them, and so kill Him. But they did not; and after a time Herod died, and Joseph returned, with Jesus and Mary, to Nazareth.

Question 6 ❖ Why did Saint Joseph take Mary and Jesus to Egypt?

_____

Question 7 ❖ What did Herod do after he realized the three Wise Men had not told him where Jesus was born?

_____

Question 8 ❖ Why was Moses never allowed to enter the Promised Land?

_____

The Saints

Saint Anne

Saint Anne is the Mother of Our Blessed Lady. God chose Anne and her husband Joachim to be Mary's parents. God gave Anne the wonderful privilege of caring for His Mother, Mary.

Anne and her husband belonged to the house of David. They came from Galilee and lived in Nazareth.

Since early Christian times churches were dedicated in honor of Saint Anne. The Fathers of the church frequently extolled her virtues, sanctity and privileges.

Saint Anne is the Patroness of Christian mothers and her Feast Day is the 26th of July.

Question 9 ❖ Who is the mother of our Blessed Lady?

_____

Question 10 ❖ Who is the father of Our Blessed Mother?

_____

Question 11 ❖ To what Order did St Thomas Aquinas belong?

_____

The Rosary

The First Glorious Mystery - The Resurrection
Three days after the saddest day in the history of the world comes the most glorious day. Our Lord Jesus Christ, after having been scourged, crowned with thorns, mocked, nailed to a cross and pierced by a lance rises gloriously from the tomb in a transfigured (resurrected) body. This Resurrection proved that Jesus was not only a perfect man, but that He was truly God. Saint Paul said that if Christ did not rise from the dead our faith would be in vain. But Our Lord did rise from the dead and there were many witnesses.

Let us ask in this mystery of the Rosary for a stronger Faith in God. He has shown us how good and powerful He is. Let us show Him how we can be strong and believe in Him even in difficult times.

The Second Glorious Mystery - The Ascension
For forty days after Jesus rose from the dead, He appeared to His disciples, teaching them and preparing them for the coming of the Holy Ghost. On the fortieth day, with His Blessed Mother and all the disciples present, He promised them that He would be with the Church until the end of the world, and then He arose into the clouds, disappearing from their view. His last words were: "Go, teach all nations, and baptize them in the Name of the Father and of the Son and of the Holy Ghost." In this mystery, we should think of heaven and we should desire to meet Jesus in heaven when we die. We know the way to do this is by following the laws of God and always trying to please Jesus and His Blessed Mother.

Question 12 ❖ What did the Resurrection of Jesus prove?

Question 13 ❖ When praying the First Glorious Mystery, what should we especially ask for?

Question 14 ❖ How many days after the Resurrection did Jesus ascend into Heaven?

Question 15 ❖ Who was present when Jesus arose into heaven?

Level 2 - Lesson 9

General

The Seven Corporal Works of Mercy

To Give Drink to the Thirsty

Our Lord said that a cup of cold water given in His Name shall not go unrewarded. Like the first Corporal Works of Mercy, whenever we give food or drink to those in need, we are showing Our Lord that we really love our neighbor. And a true love for our neighbor is proof of our love for God.

We don't often see people in the street who are dying of thirst, but there are examples when we can put this work of mercy into practice. Parents do it all the time.

Little children would not survive long if they were not given something to drink.

Sometimes you help your mother or father by feeding or giving drink to your little brothers or sisters.

Each time you do this, in a true Catholic spirit, you are giving drink to the thirsty; you are doing a corporal works of mercy, and so you are pleasing God.

Question 16 ❖ Give an example of how you could give drink to the thirsty?

_____

Question 17 ❖ When we do a Corporal works of Mercy, we are showing God that we love Him and who else?

_____

Lesson 10

Level 2

Post Communion Level

Catechism

Actual Sin

32. **Is original sin the only kind of sin?**

Original sin is not the only kind of sin; there is another kind, called actual sin, which we ourselves commit.

33. **What is actual sin?**

Actual sin is any willful thought, desire, word, action or omission forbidden by the law of God.

34. **How many kinds of actual sin are there?**

There are two kinds of actual sin: mortal sin and venial sin.

There are two different types of sin, Original Sin and Actual Sin. Original Sin, as we learnt in the last lesson, is the sin that we all inherit from Adam and Eve when we are born. To have this sin taken from our soul we must be baptized. Actual Sin is different. It is the sin that we, ourselves commit.

There are two types of Actual Sin, they are Mortal Sin and Venial Sin. Mortal Sin is so serious that it deprives the soul of grace and if we die in the state of Mortal Sin, we will lose God forever and be sent to hell. Venial Sin is a lesser sin, (but remember, all sin offends God). It wounds the soul and we should avoid it at all costs.

Question 1 ❖ Is original sin the only kind of sin?

_____

Question 2 ❖ How many kinds of actual sin are there?

_____

Question 3 ❖ What has happened to us on account of the sin of Adam?

_____

Level 2 - Lesson 10

Prayer

The Fatima Prayer to the Holy Trinity

In this lesson we are going to learn the Fatima Prayer to the Holy Trinity. The Angel of Peace taught the children this prayer in 1916, the year before Our Lady appeared to them.

O Most Holy Trinity, Father, Son
and Holy Ghost,
I adore Thee profoundly.
I offer Thee the most precious
Body, Blood, Soul
and Divinity of Jesus Christ,
present in all the Tabernacles
of the World,
in reparation for the outrages,
sacrilegious and indifference
by which He is offended
and through the infinite merits of
His Most Sacred Heart, and the
Immaculate Heart of Mary,
I beg the conversion of poor sinners.

Question 4 ❖ To whom is this prayer being prayed?

_____

Question 5 ❖ Who taught the children this prayer to the Holy Trinity?

_____

Bible Story

Jesus in the Temple

In those days there was a great feast in the Temple at Jerusalem every year, and people from all parts of the country used to go to Jerusalem for this feast. Joseph and Mary used to go, too, every year. The Child Jesus was a beautiful Boy, and growing strong, and tall, and more lovely every year. When He was twelve years old Joseph and Mary took Him to Jerusalem for one of these feasts, and a great number of their friends and relations went too, and they all stayed there some days.

On their way home again they missed Jesus; Mary thought He was with Joseph, and Joseph thought He was with Mary. When they found it was not so, they said: "Oh, He is with our relations;" but when they asked their friends, they said: "No, we have not seen Him." So Mary and Joseph went back to Jerusalem and looked about for Him for three days. At last they went into the Temple, and there they found Jesus sitting down with a number of learned people around Him. He was listening to them and asking them questions and answering them in a wise and clever way; so wise that all these learned men were surprised.

When Mary saw Him, she said to Him: "Son, why have you done this to us? Your father and I were so upset that we lost you" Then Jesus answered, and said to them: "Why did you think I was lost; did you not know I must be about My Father's house?" Mary and Joseph could not understand why He spoke that way to them, but Mary kept all these words in her heart to ponder them. Then Jesus went back with them to Nazareth, and was subject to them; that is, He obeyed them in all things.

Question 6 ❖ For how many days did Mary and Joseph search for Jesus?

_____

Question 7 ❖ Where was Jesus and what was He doing?

_____

Question 8 ❖ When Jesus went back with Mary and Joseph to Nazareth, what did He do?

_____

The Saints

Saint Dominic

Saint Dominic was born in Spain. He was a very brave and smart young man. Saint Dominic had a great devotion to the poor, it is said that he sold many of his books and even his clothes so that he could give the money to the poor. What a holy and generous man!

In the time of Saint Dominic, there were a lot of evil men called Albigenses. They committed terrible crimes against all those who loved Our Lord Jesus Christ. They burned churches and good people's homes, but worse yet, they even killed Catholics, especially priests and nuns.

Saint Dominic decided to call together an army of peace to fight these men. So he called many good, Catholic men and women together. They dressed in a white habit and were called the "Order of Preachers", or as we call them nowadays, Dominican's. Like a missionary, Saint Dominic and his priests and nuns went all over the world to teach the Catholic faith.

He told his Dominicans to "Pray for sinners". Saint Dominic fought with a powerful weapon that was given to him by Our Blessed Mother herself, it was the weapon of the Holy Rosary. Therefore Saint Dominic and his holy men and women won their fight against the enemies of the Church.

Saint Dominic feast Day is August 4th.

Question 9 ❖ What was the name of the Order that Saint Dominic started?

_____

Question 10 ❖ What special weapon did Mary give St Dominic?

_____

Question 11 ❖ When is Saint Dominic's feast day?

_____

The Rosary

The Third Glorious Mystery - The Descent of the Holy Ghost

After Our Lord had ascended into heaven the Apostles and Our Blessed Mother assembled in the Upper Room and prayed for the coming of the Holy Ghost.

The Apostles, who were very scared and confused were comforted by Mary as they awaited the coming of the Third Person of the Blessed Trinity.

The Holy Ghost appeared as tongues of fire and immediately, the Apostles received the gifts of the Holy Ghost (the same gifts we will receive at our Confirmation).

They went out immediately and preached to the many people who were there and on that very day 3,000 people were baptized. This was the first Pentecost Sunday.

Let us ask in this mystery that the Holy Ghost fills us with love and zeal for the Faith.

Question 12 ❖ How did the Holy Ghost appear to Our Lady and the Apostles?

Question 13 ❖ How many people were baptized on the first Pentecost Sunday?

Question 14 ❖ How many days after the Resurrection did Jesus ascend into heaven?

Level 2 - Lesson 10

General

The Seven Corporal Works of Mercy

To Clothe the Naked

There are so many poor people in the world who don't even have enough money to buy clothes for themselves. They are cold in winter and cannot even cover their poor bodies.

We can help these people. Instead of throwing away our clothes that we have grown out of, we can give them to some needy family or to a charity that gives out clothes to poor people. We can even send over some clothes to poorer countries; these people would be so happy to receive our clothes to wear.

There was once a great Saint Martin of Tours, who was a soldier. He saw a poor beggar by the side of the road, so he got down from his horse and tore his beautiful cloak in half and gave it to the beggar.

Whenever we give others some clothes, we should do it in a spirit of charity. We might even spend some of our own money and buy some new clothes for the poor.

Remember, when we are charitable towards our neighbor, we are really showing our love for God.

Question 15 ❖ When we do acts of charity towards our neighbor, to Whom are we really showing our love?

_____

Question 16 ❖ Which great Saint once gave half his coat to a poor man?

_____

Lesson 11

Level 2

Post Communion Level

Catechism

Mortal Sin

35.   **What is mortal sin?**

Mortal sin is a grievous offence against the law of God.

36.   **Why is this sin called mortal?**

This sin is called mortal because it takes away the life of the soul.

37.   **What three things are necessary to make a sin mortal?**

To make a sin mortal these three things are necessary:
first, *the thought, desire, word, action or omission must be seriously wrong or considered seriously wrong;*
second, *the sinner must know it is seriously wrong;*
third, *the sinner must fully consent to it.*

It is so important to learn about Mortal Sin. There is only one thing that offends God and that is sin! Mortal Sin is so serious that it takes away God's grace from our souls (the life of the soul). Oh, what a tragedy to die in this state!

We must learn exactly what a mortal sin is so we know exactly what to avoid. That is why, Question 37 is so important. Learn it well and understand the three things that make a sin mortal. Why? So that you never ever commit one.

Question 1 ❖ What is mortal sin?

_____

Question 2 ❖ What three things are necessary to make a sin mortal?

_____

_____

_____

Level 2 - Lesson 11

Prayer

Prayer to our Guardian Angel

When we were born, God gave each one of us a guardian angel to watch over us and protect us for all of our lives. He is our very good friend. We should pray to him every day. Learn the prayer to your Guardian Angel and pray it every morning and every night.

Angel of God
My guardian dear
To Whom His love
Commits me here
Ever this day
Be at my side
To light and guard
To rule and guide. Amen

Question 3 ❖ To whom are we speaking when we make the sign of the Cross?

_____

Question 4 ❖ What are the two most important times of the day we should pray?

_____

Bible Story

The Baptism of Jesus

A good many years had now passed, and John, the son of Zachary, who had been living all this time in a lonely place; the desert, praying to God, was told by God that now he should tell the people what to do. So he left the desert, and came to the river Jordan, the same river that rolled back for the Jews hundreds of years before.

Here John called all the people about him, and told them of God: that they should never more be wicked. After he had baptized them, he told them such holy things, that at last the people said that he must be the Christ. But John was pained at this, and he told them that he was not worthy to untie the shoes of Christ. This meant that even as a servant he was not worthy to serve Jesus Christ.

One day Jesus also came to the river Jordan to be baptized by John. When John saw Jesus coming, he said: "Behold the Lamb of God, behold Him who taketh away the sins of the world." After the baptism a wonderful thing took place. The sky opened, and the Holy Ghost, in the shape of a dove, flew down to Jesus, and a voice was heard by the people saying: "This is My beloved Son, in Whom I am well pleased." Jesus at this time was about thirty years old.

Question 5 ❖ How old was Jesus when he was baptized?

_____

Question 6 ❖ Who baptized Jesus?

_____

Question 7 ❖ When Saint John the Baptist saw Jesus coming, what did he say?

_____

Question 8 ❖ For how many days did Mary and Joseph search for Jesus when He was lost?

_____

The Saints

Saint Angela Merici

Angela Merici was a lovely young Italian woman. She knew many poor girls. Most of them did not know about Jesus Christ. Many of them had never heard much about the lovely Mother of God. And many of them were sinful and bad. But Angela knew this was because no one had taught them about Jesus and Mary.

She helped sinful girls to become good once more. She built houses where they could live and be safe from temptation. She found fine, pure wise young women to teach the children. She wanted sinless girls to help save sinful girls. She took Saint Ursula for her patron. Then she invited good young women and pure sweet girls to help her. They became the first Ursuline Sisters. They went all over the world teaching and helping little children and girls and young women.
Today there are thousands of these Sisters. They all call Saint Angela their Patroness and Holy Mother.

Saint Angela Merici feast day is June 1st.

Question 9 ◆ From what country did Saint Angela Merici come?

___

Question 10 ◆ Who did Saint Angela help?

___

Question 11 ◆ What was the name of the Order Saint Angela Merici started?

___

Question 12 ◆ What special weapon did Mary give St Dominic?

___

The Rosary

The Fourth Glorious Mystery - The Assumption

Our Blessed Mother lived for a number of years after Jesus died. Saint John, the Apostle looked after her as Jesus asked him to do from the Cross.

But there came a time when Jesus wanted to take His Blessed Mother to heaven, so He sent His angels down to the earth and they carried Mary to heaven. What rejoicing there was at that time in heaven! The angels and saints were so happy to see Mary in heaven, and Mary herself was full of eternal joy with her Son.

When we pray this decade of the Rosary, we should ask for the grace of a happy death. Our goal is heaven, and if we lead good lives and die a holy death, we will spend all eternity with God, with Mary and with all the angels and saints.

The Fifth Glorious Mystery - The Coronation

When Mary was taken up into heaven by the angels, she was taken to the throne of God, and there, in the presence of all the angels and saints, she was crowned queen of heaven and earth. What an honor! Let us remember to always have a true devotion to Mary. If we love the Mother of God, she will take us by the hand and lead us to her Son, Jesus. In this final mystery of the Rosary let us ask Our Blessed Lady to protect us always from the snares of the devil and to guide us to heaven.

Question 13 ❖ Who carried Mary into heaven?

_____

Question 14 ❖ Who looked after Mary after Jesus died?

_____

Question 15 ❖ God crowned Mary as what?

_____

Question 16 ❖ To whom should we have a true devotion?

_____

Level 2 - Lesson 11

General

The Seven Corporal Works of Mercy

To Visit the Imprisoned

This works of Mercy brings to mind both convicted criminals and the innocent victims of persecution. Those who visit prisoners in jail and give them instruction and/or material help are doing a works of mercy.

It is often not possible to visit those in prison, especially as children, but we can extend charity to them in other ways. We can send good books, newspapers, magazines etc. to the jail chaplains, who can distribute them. We can pray for those in jail and especially pray for those priests and Catholics who have been unjustly imprisoned around the world, just for being Catholic.

Question 17 ❖ What are two ways we can help those in prison?

_____

Question 18 ❖ List the four Corporal Works of Mercy.

_____

_____

_____

_____

Lesson 12

Level 2

Post Communion Level

Catechism

Venial Sin

38. What is venial sin?

Venial sin is a less serious offence against the law of God.

39. How can a sin be venial?

A sin can be venial in two ways:

first, *when the evil done is not seriously wrong;*

second, *when the evil done is seriously wrong, but the sinner sincerely believes it is only slightly wrong, or does not give full consent to it.*

Sometimes when we read about venial sin we think or say, "Oh, it is only a venial sin!" Well, it is true that venial sin is a lesser sin and it is true that venial sin only wounds our soul and does not destroy God's life in us...BUT…. All sin offends God! And we must avoid it at all costs.

If we think little of venial sin, and do not worry about committing them, they will soon lead us into mortal sin. We must avoid all sin, not only to avoid the punishment we will receive, but to show God how much we love Him.

Question 1 ❖ How can a sin be venial?

_____

Question 2 ❖ Why is mortal sin mortal?

_____

Level 2 - Lesson 12

Prayer

The Fatima Sacrifice Prayer

O my Jesus, it is for love of You, for the conversion of sinners, and in reparation for the offenses committed against the Immaculate Heart of Mary.

This prayer can be said when making any sacrifice. It offers your sacrifice, however big or small, firstly, for the love of Our Dear Saviour, secondly, for the conversion of sinners (this is something Our Lady asked us to pray and make sacrifices for at Fatima), and thirdly, for all of the offenses committed against her Immaculate Heart.

It is not very easy to make sacrifices, even adults find it difficult. Let us try to be like Saint Therese, who made lots of little sacrifices daily! In that way, it will help make us stronger to face the big sacrifices we must make, for the love of Jesus and Mary, when we are older. Remember if you find it hard to make sacrifices, ask Jesus to help you, He will always help if you ask for it. He made the biggest sacrifice, that was dying on the cross, and He made it just for us. Let us help Our Lord by sharing some of the pain and suffering He underwent.

By making sacrifices we can help to ease some of His pain.

Question 3 ❖ By praying the Sacrifice Prayer, what are the three things you can offer up your sacrifices for?

_____

Question 4 ❖ Which Saint should we try and imitate who made many little sacrifices each day?

_____

Bible Story

Jesus' First Miracle

Jesus loved His Mother Mary very much, and He did what she asked Him to do. There was one day a wedding at a place called Cana, and Jesus and Mary were asked to attend. At the feast all the wine was used, for there was not enough, and when Mary saw this, she told Jesus that there was no wine. Jesus did not want to use His power yet; but He could not deny His Mother, as we shall see.

He said to Mary: "Woman, what is it to Me and to thee?" But Mary knew in her heart that Jesus would do what she wanted. So she said to the servant-men who were waiting at the table: "Do whatever he tells you" (These were the last words Our Lady spoke in the Bible)

Now, in the room there were six large stone jars, with a little water in them, and Jesus, calling to Him the servants, said to them: "Fill the water-pots with water." And they filled them up to the brim. Then Jesus said: "Draw the water out now and take it to the chief steward;" and they did; but the man did not know, when he had tasted it, where the wine had come from, for Jesus had changed the water into wine. And the chief steward said: "Our host has kept the best wine for the last."

This is the beginning of miracles Jesus did in Cana of Galilee, and manifested His glory, and His disciples believed in Him. Jesus then went to His own city, Nazareth.

Question 5 ❖ Where did Jesus perform His first miracle?

_____

Question 6 ❖ Who asked Jesus to perform His first miracle?

_____

Question 7 ❖ What were the last words Our Lady spoke in the Bible?

_____

The Saints

Saint Rose of Lima

After the discovery of the New World, the first South American Saint was born in Lima, capital of Peru, Saint Rose.

Rose got her name because one day her face was seen transfigured with all the beauty of a rose.

While still a little child, she vowed to live a life of virginity (that is, not to get married, but spend her whole life loving God and working for Him).

She became a Third Order Dominican. After spending her life in prayer and making many sacrifices, she died at the age of 31. She had dedicated herself to saving souls and had become a model of patience and purity.

Saint Rose of Lima feast day is August 30th

Question 8 ❖ In what town of Peru was Saint Rose born?

_____

Question 9 ❖ How old was Saint Rose when she died?

_____

Question 10 ❖ Saint Rose was a model of what two things?

_____

The Rosary

October, the Month of the Holy Rosary

The Church specifies certain months of the year to certain devotions. June is the Month of the Sacred Heart, November is the Month of the Holy Souls and October is the Month of the Holy Rosary.

We have just completed several lessons learning about the various Mysteries of the Rosary, from the time the Angel Gabriel came to Nazareth to ask Mary to be the Mother of God, right up to the Crowning of Our Blessed Lady as Queen of heaven and earth.

During the Month of October, we think in a special way of this wonderful prayer. We try even harder to say it every day and say it well. Our Lady herself appeared for the last time to the three children of Fatima during October. It was at this October apparition that the Great Miracle of the sun took place.

So during this wonderful month, remember to pray the Rosary everyday with full attention and devotion.

Question 11 ❖ Which is the month of the Holy Rosary?

_____

Question 12 ❖ What miracle took place in Fatima during the October apparition?

_____

Question 13 ❖ Who carried Mary into heaven?

_____

Level 2 - Lesson 12

General

The Seven Corporal Works of Mercy

To Shelter the Homeless

Giving shelter to a stranger or a home to the homeless is a splendid work of mercy. Generous and unselfish people make room for an aged parent, a neighbor in distress, a friend stricken by a disaster such as a fire or flood. To adopt a child, or to offer a homeless child temporary shelter is especially pleasing to God.

Charitable organizations under the direction of the Church provide orphanages, homes for the dying, old age homes and nursing homes. People working in these homes (especially the volunteers) are helping to shelter the homeless.

As a young child, it is difficult to do many of these things, but you can desire to do them when you are older, and you can help your parents willingly if they do any of the above.

Question 14 ❖ When we do acts of charity towards our neighbor, to whom are we really showing our love?

_____

Question 15 ❖ List two ways you could shelter the homeless?

_____

_____

Lesson 13

Level 2

Post Communion Level

Catechism

The Incarnation

40.   Did God abandon man after Adam fell into sin?

God did not abandon man after Adam fell into sin, but promised to send into the world a Saviour to free man from his sins and to reopen to him the gates of heaven.

41.   Who is the Saviour of all men?

The Saviour of all men is Jesus Christ.

42.   What is the chief teaching of the Catholic Church about Jesus Christ?

The chief teaching of the Catholic Church about Jesus Christ is that He is God made man.

The word Incarnation means becoming flesh; in other words, becoming a man. Yes, God became a man. The Second Person of the Blessed Trinity, Jesus Christ, became a man for us, that He might suffer and die upon the Cross, to make up for the sin of Adam.

What a great love Our Lord has for us! We call Jesus our Saviour because, through His death, He has opened the gates of heaven. Let us never forget to thank Our Lord for all He has done for us.

Question 1   ❖   Did God abandon man after Adam fell into sin?

_____

Question 2   ❖   What is the chief teaching of the Catholic Church about Jesus Christ?

_____

Question 3   ❖   What is venial sin?

_____

Prayer

The Fatima Eucharist Prayer

Most Holy Trinity,
I adore Thee!
My God, I love Thee in the most
Blessed Sacrament.

This lovely prayer can be said at any time, but especially at the Holy Sacrifice of the Mass, during the Consecration, or at the Benediction, when you are praying in the Church, or even when you are at home.

Think of Jesus in the Tabernacle, a prisoner of love, waiting for you to come and visit Him. Remember the story of The Agony in the Garden? All of the Apostles fell asleep and Jesus was suffering alone, hoping that they would wake and pray with Him. But nobody did. Poor Jesus!

"Will you not watch one hour with Me?" Let us never leave Him. When you have the opportunity, kneel in front of the Blessed Sacrament, think of how much Jesus loves us and then say this beautiful prayer that the Angel of Portugal taught the three children at Fatima!

Question 4 ❖ When is a good time to pray the Fatima Eucharist Prayer?

_____

Question 5 ❖ Who waits in the tabernacle for you to come to pray to him?

_____

Question 6 ❖ Write out the Fatima sacrifice prayer.

_____

_____

Bible Story

Jesus Calms the Storm

One day Jesus said to His disciples: "Let us go over to the other side of the lake." They had been teaching the people near a lake called Galilee and He got into a little ship with His disciples.

After they had been out on the water a short time, Jesus, who was tired, went to sleep. When He was asleep a storm of wind came on and the boat began to fill with water, and they were in danger. The disciples, being afraid, went to Jesus and awoke Him, and said: "Master, we will perish." So Jesus, getting up, told the wind to be quiet and the sea also, and it became quite and calm.

Question 7 ❖ What was the lake upon which Jesus and His disciples were in the boat?

_____

Question 8 ❖ What was the miracle that Jesus performed?

_____

Question 9 ❖ Where did Jesus perform His first miracle?

_____

The Saints

All Saints

The first day of November is the feast of All Saints. We think of the Saints not only on this special feast day, but all through the year. Everyone who goes to heaven is a Saint – just think of that, isn't it wonderful! One day, we too, can be Saints in heaven, if we serve God well on earth; (we may have to spend some time in Purgatory though, to be pure enough for heaven).

We can become saints much more quickly if we love Jesus and Mary more than anyone else – more than our parents, our very special friends or anyone!.

Let us try to think what a wonderful place heaven must be; better than anything here on the earth. We can look at beautiful pictures, read beautiful stories, visit interesting places, look at the birds, trees, flowers, fishes, the stars and so many wonderful things God has made. Yet none of these things can compare even a tiny bit to what God's Kingdom in heaven is like.
The most important thing about heaven is that we see God and all His angels and saints, and we will be happy for ever and ever.

So on the feast of All Saints, we think of all the saints we know and of the many others we do not know. Perhaps even some of our relatives or friends who have died are already in heaven and are celebrating their feast day – All Saint's Day. So let us pray to them to help us live better lives that one day we will join them in the happiness of heaven.

All Saints Feast Day is the 1st of November

Question 10 ❖ What date is the Feast of All Saints?

_____

Question 11 ❖ Do we know the names of all the Saints in heaven?

_____

Question 12 ❖ In what town of Peru was Saint Rosa born?

_____

The Rosary

The Story of Fatima – Part 1

OUR LADY OF FATIMA
Pray for Us

Our Blessed Lady appeared six times to the children at Fatima, in 1917. Lucy was then 10, Francisco 9 and Jacinta 7. At noon, on the 13th May, the children knelt to say the Rosary in the meadow where they were tending the sheep. The beautiful Lady, dressed in white appeared to them. She told the children not to be afraid. She was from heaven. She asked them to come to the same place at the same time for six months in a row. At every visit, she asked the children to say the Rosary every day.

On the 13th June, Our Lady gave them the same message – pray the Rosary every day. The Lady asked Lucy to learn to read. Later she would tell them what she wanted. In her right hand she held a heart surrounded by thorns which pierced it. It was a symbol of the Immaculate Heart of Mary, outraged by the sins of the world, and that she wished for reparation (making up for the sins). The following month, on the 13th of July Our Lady promised the children there would be a miracle in October and that she would tell them who she was. She also showed the children a vision of how terrible hell is and she said that if men did not stop offending God many terrible things would happen in the world.

Question 13 ❖ How many times did Our Lady appear to the children?

_____

Question 14 ❖ In July, what did Our Lady show the children?

_____

Question 15 ❖ What was the message that Our Lady gave to the children every month?

_____

Question 16 ❖ Who carried Mary into heaven?

_____

Level 2 - Lesson 13

General

The Seven Corporal Works of Mercy

To Visit the Sick

We are never without the opportunity to visit the sick. If we have members of our family who are sick, we can help comfort them, read to them or just talk to them. Sometimes a friend might be sick at home or in hospital. With our parents permission we could visit them. Sometimes it is very lonely in hospital, so a visit from a friend is usually much appreciated.

Sometimes, at school or with a group of other children, you could organize to go to a hospital and sing Christmas carols for the old, sick people, or do a little play or skit for them. This would take their minds off their sickness and make them feel a lot better.

Question 17 ❖ Name two places where we can visit the sick?

_____

Question 18 ❖ If you visited old people in a hospital, what could you do to make them feel better?

_____

Lesson 14

Level 2

Post Communion Level

Catechism

The Incarnation

43. Is Jesus Christ more than one Person?

No, Jesus Christ is only one Person; and that Person is the second Person of the Blessed Trinity.

44. How many natures has Jesus Christ?

Jesus Christ has two natures: the nature of God and the nature of man.

45. When was Christ born?

Christ was born of the Blessed Virgin Mary on Christmas Day, in Bethlehem, more than two thousand years ago.

We learnt last lesson that the Incarnation was when Jesus became man. This lesson we have a very important, but difficult truth to learn. Jesus, the Second Person of the Blessed Trinity has two natures, that of God and Man, but He is only one Person. This is not easy to understand, but it is very important.

Question 1 ❖ Is Jesus Christ more than one Person?

_____

Question 2 ❖ How many natures has Jesus Christ?

_____

Question 3 ❖ Who is the Saviour of all men?

_____

Level 2 - Lesson 14

Prayer

Eternal Rest

Eternal rest grant unto them, O Lord, and let perpetual light shine upon them. May the souls of the faithful departed, through the mercy of God, rest in peace. Amen.

This lesson we are revising a prayer we learnt in Level One. This prayer is so important, remember to pray this prayer often to help the souls in Purgatory! Make a habit of every time you pass by a Cemetery, to say this prayer for the Holy Souls, and perhaps one day, if you go to purgatory they will repay you for the prayers you said for them and how could Our dear God refuse the prayer of one of His Saints? (although we pray with all our hearts we go straight to heaven).

Question 4 ❖ Who are we praying for when we pray the Eternal Rest?

_____

Question 5 ❖ When is a good time to pray for the Holy Souls?

_____

Bible Story

The Loaves and Fishes

A great crowd of five thousand and more followed Jesus to a lonely place, far away from a town, to hear him preach. It was evening, and no one had anything to eat. So the disciples came to Jesus, and said to Him: "Send away the people, that they may go to the towns and buy food." But Jesus said to them: "You give them to eat." And they said: "We have no more than five loaves and two fishes, unless we go and buy food for all the people." Jesus said: "Make them sit down in groups of fifty." And so the disciples did as Jesus asked.

And Jesus took the five loaves and the two fishes, and He looked up to heaven and blessed them; and He broke the bread and gave it to His disciples to give to the people. And all these five thousand men had so much to eat from the five loaves and two fishes that when they had enough, twelve baskets were filled with the broken pieces.

This was a great wonder, and it was done to show us what Jesus does on our altars.

Question 6 ❖ How many loaves and fishes did Jesus have to feed the 5,000?

_____

Question 7 ❖ After everyone had eaten, how many baskets of leftovers were collected by the Apostles?

_____

Question 8 ❖ What does this miracle represent?

_____

The Saints

Saint Nicholas

Saint Nicholas was born many years ago – in the third century. He became a priest when he was older, and eventually was appointed abbot of a monastery.

Nicholas was always very generous to the poor. He was the special protector of the innocent and the wronged.

Once he heard that a man became very poor and was going to allow his three daughters to live a life of sin. He went out by night, flung a bag of gold into the window of the sleeping father, and hurried away. Later, the father said to Saint Nicholas, you are my helper. You have delivered my soul and my daughters' from hell."

Saint Nicholas is regarded as the special patron of children; the word Santa Claus comes from his name. He died at Myra in the year 342.

Saint Nicholas feast day is on December 6th.

Question 9 ❖ When is the feast of Saint Nicholas?

_____

Question 10 ❖ Of whom is Saint Nicholas the patron?

_____

Question 11 ❖ Saint Nicholas was very generous to whom?

_____

The Rosary

The Story of Fatima – Part 2

The Mayor of the district kidnapped the children so they could not go on the 13th August. There were big crowds beginning to gather on the days of the expected apparitions, and he wanted the people to think that the children were making up the stories about the Lady.

Our Lady did appear to the children when they returned from gaol. A few days later, on September 13th, the big crowd said the Rosary with the children. The Lady's message this time was: Continue to say the Rosary in order to end the war. In October Our Lord will come, and Our Lady of Sorrows and Our Lady of Mt. Carmel. Saint Joseph will appear with the Child Jesus to bless the world.

On October 13th, 1917, although there was torrential rain, a huge crowd of people estimated to be over 70, 000 came, they knelt in the mud and humbly prayed the Rosary with the children. Everything happened as Our Blessed Lady predicted with a great miracle of the sun spinning towards the earth and then it's return to the sky. There were also the apparitions as Our Lady had promised, that only the children saw.

Another miracle happened after the sun shone and it was back on course, the crowd found that their formally sodden clothes were dry and comfortable without trace of mud or rain and many people were cured.

Question 12 ❖ Did the promised miracle happen on October 13th?

_____

Question 13 ❖ How many times did Our Lady appear to the three children?

_____

General

The Seven Corporal Works of Mercy

To Bury the Dead

When a person dies, his soul goes to heaven, hell or purgatory. His body is buried in the ground (and rots), where it waits until the end of the world when it will once again join its soul.

It is a corporal works of mercy to ensure that a person gets a Catholic burial. If the family of the deceased cannot afford a burial, it is meritorious to help them financially to do so.

Question 14 ❖ What happens to the body after it is buried?

_____

Question 15 ❖ What could you do to help a family who could not afford to bury their relative?

_____

Question 16 ❖ If you visited old people in a hospital, what could you do to make them feel better?

_____

Lesson 15

Level 2

Post Communion Level

Catechism

This is the last lesson of the year and is different to all other lessons, as there are no new questions, nor is there any new work to learn, nor is there a test to complete. It is a revision lesson. It is a summary of all you have learned this year.

There are two reasons why such a summary of your work is important. Firstly, it gives you the opportunity to review all the things you have already studied, so that you have a better knowledge of your work and you will therefore be more pleasing to God. Secondly, it will serve as a good preparation for Level 3.

Catechism

1. **Who made us?**
   God made us

2. **Who is God?**
   God is the Supreme Being, infinitely perfect, Who made all things and keeps them in existence.

3. **Why did God make us?**
   God made us to show forth His goodness and to share with us His everlasting happiness in heaven.

4. **What must we do to gain the happiness of heaven?**
   To gain the happiness of heaven we must know, love and serve God in this world.

5. **From whom do we learn to know, love and serve God?**
   We learn to know, love and serve God from Jesus Christ, the Son of God, Who teaches us through the Catholic Church.

6. **Where do we find the chief truths taught by Jesus Christ through the Catholic Church?**
   We find the chief truths taught by Jesus Christ through the Catholic Church in the Apostles' Creed.

Catechism

Level 2 - Lesson 15

7. **Say the Apostles' Creed**

I believe in God, the Father Almighty, Creator of heaven and earth; And in Jesus Christ, His only Son, Our Lord; Who was conceived by the Holy Ghost, born of the Virgin Mary, suffered under Pontius Pilate was crucified, died and was buried. He descended into hell; the third day He arose again from the dead; He ascended into heaven, sitteth at the right hand of God, the Father Almighty, from thence He shall come to judge the living and the dead. I believe in the Holy Ghost, the Holy Catholic Church, the communion of saints, the forgiveness of sins, the resurrection of the body, and life everlasting. Amen.

8. **What do we mean when we say that God is the Supreme Being?**
When we say that God is the Supreme Being we mean that He is above all creatures.

9. **What do we mean when we say that God is eternal?**
When we say that God is eternal we mean that He always was and always will be, and that He always remains the same.

10. **What do we mean when we say that God is all-Knowing?**
When we say that God is all-knowing we mean that He knows all things, past, present, and future, even our most secret thoughts, words and actions.

11. **What do we mean when we say God is all-Present?**
When we say that God is all-present we mean that He is everywhere.

12. **Does God see us?**
God sees us and watches over us with loving care.

13. **What do we mean when we say that God is almighty?**
When we say that God is almighty we mean that He can do all things.

14. **Is there only one God?**
Yes, there is only one God

15. **How many Persons are there in God?**

In God, there are three Divine Persons – the Father, the Son and the Holy Ghost

16. **What do we mean by the Blessed Trinity?**

By the Blessed Trinity we mean one and the same God in three Divine Persons.

Catechism

17. What do we mean when we say that God is the Creator of heaven and earth?
When we say that God is the Creator of heaven and earth we mean that He made all things from nothing.

18. Which are the chief creatures of God?
The chief creatures of God are angels and men.

19. What are angels?
Angels are created spirits without bodies.

20. Did all the angels remain faithful to God?
Not all the angels remained faithful to God; some of them sinned.

21. What happened to the angels who remained faithful to God?
The angels who remained faithful to God entered into the eternal happiness of heaven, and these are called good angels.

22. How do the good angels help us?
The good angels help us by praying for us, by acting as messengers from God to us, and by serving as our guardian angels.

23. What happened to the angels who did not remain faithful to God?
The angels who did not remain faithful to God were cast into hell, and these are called bad angels, or devils.

24. What is man?
Man is a creature of God composed of body and soul, and made in the image and likeness of God.

25. Who were the first man and woman?
The first man and woman were Adam and Eve.

26. What commandment did God give Adam and Eve?
God gave Adam and Eve the commandment not to eat of the fruit of a certain tree that grew in the Garden of Paradise.

27. Did Adam and Eve obey the Commandment of God?
Adam and Eve did not obey the commandment of God, but ate of the forbidden fruit.

Catechism

28. **What happened to Adam and Eve on account of their sin?**
On account of their sin Adam and Eve lost sanctifying grace and the right to heaven, and were driven from the Garden of Eden.

29. **What has happened to us on account of the sin of Adam?**
On account of the sin of Adam we come into the world without grace, and we inherit his punishment.

30. **What is this sin in us called?**
This sin in us is called original sin.

31. **Was any human person ever free from original sin?**
The Blessed Virgin Mary was free from original sin, and this favor is called her Immaculate Conception.

32. **Is original sin the only kind of sin?**
Original sin is not the only kind of sin; there is another kind, called actual sin, which we ourselves commit.

33. **What is actual sin?**
Actual sin is any willful thought, desire, word, action or omission forbidden by the law of God.

34. **How many kinds of actual sin are there?**
There are two kinds of actual sin: mortal sin and venial sin.

35. **What is mortal sin?**
Mortal sin is a grievous offence against the law of God.

36. **Why is this sin called mortal?**
This sin is called mortal because it takes away the life of the soul.

37. **What three things are necessary to make a sin mortal?**
To make a sin mortal these three things are necessary:
first, *the thought, desire, word, action or omission must be seriously wrong or considered seriously wrong;*
second, *the sinner must know it is seriously wrong;*
third, *the sinner must fully consent to it.*

Catechism

38. What is venial sin?
Venial sin is a less serious offence against the law of God.

39. How can a sin be venial?
A sin can be venial in two ways:
***first**, when the evil done is not seriously wrong;*
***second**, when the evil done is seriously wrong, but the sinner sincerely believes it is only slightly wrong, or does not give full consent to it.*

40. Did God abandon man after Adam fell into sin?
God did not abandon man after Adam fell into sin, but promised to send into the world a Saviour to free man from his sins and to reopen to him the gates of heaven.

41. Who is the Saviour of all men?
The Saviour of all men is Jesus Christ.

42. What is the chief teaching of the Catholic Church about Jesus Christ?
The chief teaching of the Catholic Church about Jesus Christ is that He is God made man.

43. Is Jesus Christ more than one Person?
No, Jesus Christ is only one Person; and that Person is the second Person of the Blessed Trinity.

44. How many natures has Jesus Christ?
Jesus Christ has two natures: the nature of God and the nature of man.

45. When was Christ born?
Christ was born of the Blessed Virgin Mary on Christmas Day, in Bethlehem, more than two thousand years ago.

www.ingramcontent.com/pod-product-compliance
Lightning Source LLC
Chambersburg PA
CBHW061749290426

44108CB00028B/2929